**TED**Books

# How to Fix a Broken Heart

DR GUY WINCH

ILLUSTRATIONS BY HENN KIM

TED Books
Simon & Schuster

London   New York   Toronto   Sydney   New Delhi

First published in Great Britain by Simon & Schuster UK Ltd, 2018
A CBS COMPANY

Copyright © Dr Guy Winch, 2018

The right of Dr Guy Winch to be identified as the author of this work has been asserted in accordance with the Copyright, Designs and Patents Act, 1988.

First TED Books hardback edition February 2018

TED, the TED logo and TED Books are trademarks of TED Conference, LLC.
TED BOOKS and colophon are registered trademarks of TED Conferences, LLC.

For more information on licensing the TED talk that accompanies this book, or other content partnerships with TED, please contact TEDBooks@TED.com.

10 9 8 7 6 5 4 3 2 1

Simon & Schuster UK Ltd
1st Floor
222 Gray's Inn Road
London WC1X 8HB

www.simonandschuster.co.u
www.simonandschuster.com
www.simonandschuster.co.i

Simon & Schuster Australia,
Simon & Schuster India, Nev

The author and publishers ha
copyright-holders for permis
in the form of credits given. (

A CIP catalogue record for th
is available from the British I

Hardback ISBN: 978-1-4711-6857-4
eBook ISBN: 978-1-4711-6858-1

Illustrations by Henn Kim
Interior design by MGMT.design

Printed and bound by CPI Group (UK) Ltd, Croydon, CR0 4YY

| LEABHARLANN PHORT LÁIRGE | |
| --- | --- |
| | |
| Bertrams | 14/03/2018 |
| | |
| UE | 02321336 |

MIX
Paper from responsible sources
FSC® C020471

Simon & Schuster UK are committed to sourcing paper that is made from wood grown in sustainable forests and support the Forest Stewardship Council, the leading international forest certification organisation. Our books displaying the FSC logo are printed on FSC certified paper.

*To Louise Shimron*

# CONTENTS

INTRODUCTION   3

CHAPTER 1
How the Brokenhearted Are Abandoned   9

CHAPTER 2
When Hearts Break, Brains and Bodies Break Too   35

CHAPTER 3
The Many Mistakes That Set Us Back   56

CHAPTER 4
Healing Starts in the Mind   77

EPILOGUE
Making Emotional Pain Visible   100

# How to Fix a
# Broken Heart

In this book I use numerous case studies from my private practice. When doing so I have made efforts to disguise any identifying information. Consequently, the names of my patients as well as those of their significant others (both human and animal) have been changed. I have also tried to back up my assertions with empirical scientific studies published in top-notch scientific journals with blind peer-review acceptance procedures. I provide a select list of these texts in the References section.

The storm of heartbreak strikes like a hurricane. At times, we are alerted to its arrival by an early forecast of ominous signs. Often it catches us by surprise; a conversation that takes a startling turn or an unexpected text as we busily go about our day. Either way, when the storm touches down, it lands hard. The wind batters our sense of security and certainty. The icy rain soaks every nook and cranny of our being, from the part of us that is a capable professional to the part that's a devoted parent or a passionate artist or a weekend partier. We squint at the world through glasses tinted by emotional pain, fearing the dark clouds will never break. Unlike real hurricanes, heartbreak has no eye—it offers no reprieve and it leaves no place to take shelter. We thus remain exposed, drenched, and miserable until it passes.

These feelings and perceptions are familiar to most— virtually every one of us has or will have our heart broken at some point in our lives, whether by romantic love or by loss. Given how ubiquitous heartbreak is, it is remarkable that we know so little about how to heal it. Even more remarkable, given how personally familiar we are with the emotional devastation it causes, is that our societal attitudes toward heartbreak are so downright dismissive.

We tend to associate having a broken heart with something that happens to the young, the naïve, or the inexperienced—teenagers and young adults who have not yet felt the full weight of adult responsibilities on their shoulders. Real adults are supposed to handle such occurrences as they might any other setback or disappointment—with maturity and stoicism. Heartbreak resides firmly in the category of baseball and spilled milk—it is simply not something one cries over, or so we believe.

That is until our own heart gets broken.

For then, we will swiftly be reminded that heartbreak hurts just as much later in life as it did when we were teenagers—it evokes just as much paralyzing emotional pain and it impairs our thinking and functioning in all the same ways. We will also have to confront the unfortunate reality that unlike with our teenage experiences we had received in high school, the understanding, support, and compassion are likely to be noticeably absent.

Mirroring the lack of seriousness with which we regard it, the term *heartbreak* has itself become diluted. We declare ourselves "heartbroken" when our favorite sports team loses an important game, when the crystal vase we inherited from our grandmother slips out of our hands and shatters on the floor, or when we discover the heroine in our favorite novel fails to choose the supernatural teen suiter we hoped she would. As disappointing and upsetting as such events are, none of us would confuse them with the anguish we feel when our hearts are truly broken.

Real heartbreak is unmistakable, from the intensity of the emotional pain it causes, to the totality with which it takes over our mind and even our body. We think of nothing else. We feel nothing else. We care about nothing else. And often, we feel as if we can do nothing else except sit with the immense pain, grief, and loss.

Broken hearts come in many forms, but in this book, I have chosen to focus on two types of heartbreak that have much in common: romantic heartbreak and the heartbreak that ensues from the loss of a cherished pet. I have done so because these experiences involve a complication that is particularly difficult for the brokenhearted: They are accompanied by severe grief responses yet they are not deemed as important by society as, let's say, a formal divorce or the loss of a first-degree relative. As a result, we are often deprived of the recognition, support, and compassion afforded those whose heartbreak is considered significant.

Indeed, when a parent, child, or sibling dies, we are likely to get an outpouring of support and compassion from institutions as well as from individuals. Employers will offer us condolences, understanding, and bereavement leave when our parent dies. But they will do no such thing when our beloved dog dies, even though for some people the latter is just as profound if not more. Similarly, our boss is likely to be much more understanding of our lackluster performance once we explain we are going through a divorce than if we confess to mourning the loss of a short-term relationship, however intense and important.

Further complicating matters, the lack of empathy we receive from others is often reflected in our own attitudes. Too many of us ache with emotional pain only to then criticize ourselves for hurting. We falsely believe we should somehow *stay calm and carry on*—that we should be able to function normally, when psychologically speaking something very abnormal is going on. Now, new scientific studies are confirming what many of us already suspected: Heartbreak impacts our brain and our behavior in dramatic and unexpected ways, and that it does so regardless of our age.

One of the most unfortunate realities of heartbreak is that our "natural" responses often do us more harm than good. Many of the behaviors and habits we typically adopt to cope with heartache are likely to deepen our emotional pain, delay our recovery, and even damage our long-term mental health. Sadly, most of us have no idea what these behaviors are, how we might avoid them, or how we might break free of them once they are already ingrained. This same body of research has also illuminated effective techniques we could use to accelerate our healing. Most of us do not know what those are either.

As a psychologist who has had a private practice for over two decades, I have had a front-row seat, or rather, armchair to hundreds of heartbroken people and their struggle to heal and recover. Since my office is in the melting pot of New York City, my patients come from all over the world, and have a range of ages, gender identities, and ethnic and cultural backgrounds. And yet I learned early on that when it comes to heartbreak, these kinds of demographic factors matter not a whit. Cultural differences might influence how we react to heartbreak outwardly but what we feel inside, the pain and anguish we experience internally, is very much the same.

As most psychologists, I entered the field because I was motivated to ease the emotional and mental suffering of others. Looking back at the most dramatic and painful moments I've witnessed in my career, heartbreak was responsible for a majority of them. Yet, graduate school taught me very little, if anything, about how to fix a broken heart. So I turned to academic journals for enlightenment and advice.

Researchers have been studying heartbreak for years and their findings, albeit often written in dry and "academic" terms, have offered many insights and techniques that have helped my heartbroken patients recover more quickly. I present the best of them here, along with the stories of the patients who needed them, their unrecognized struggles, and the journey of healing on which we embarked together.

This book is an effort to bring heartbreak out of the shadows; first, so we recognize its devastating impact on people of every age, and second, so we have effective tools for self-healing.

If your heart is broken, it will definitely take time to heal. But, as you'll soon discover, how much time is now up to you.

# 1 How the Brokenhearted Are Abandoned

In my years as a clinical psychologist I have worked with hundreds of people whose heart was broken by love or loss. Anyone who has experienced a broken heart (and that is most of us) probably remembers the feeling well: the shock, the haze of unreality that makes us feel as though we must be in an alternate universe, and how disconnected we feel when we see those around us go about their lives as if nothing has happened, oblivious to the earthquake of emotional devastation that has shattered our world.

But by far, the most pronounced aspect of heartbreak is the paralyzing emotional pain it causes. Indeed, our very understanding of what it means to have a broken heart is so tightly bound to the incredible anguish it causes, the two are practically synonymous. In many ways they should be, as the story of heartbreak is a tale of emotional pain, our responses to that pain, and our efforts to recover from it.

When a patient's heart gets broken my heart always aches alongside theirs. The training and defense mechanisms that typically shield me in my daily work often fail in the face of such raw emotional agony. Perhaps I allow my defenses to fail—my way of letting the grief-stricken person before me know that I see their pain, I feel it. Because unfortunately, many people in their lives do not.

Our journey through heartbreak is determined by multiple variables: the specific nature of the relationship or loss, our fundamental character and coping styles, our individual and familial histories, the current context of our lives, and how we manage or mismanage our recovery. The last crucial variable that impacts our recovery is also the one most likely to disappoint us—our available support systems: friends and family, communities, schools, and places of employment.

## How Support Systems Fail the Heartbroken

Support systems typically play a pivotal role in recovery from loss. Consider what happens when we lose a first-degree relative. The outpouring of concern around us provides emotional validation, reassuring us the emotional pain we feel is a normative and reasonable response to our loss. Friends and family offer compassion and empathy, as well as both literal and metaphorical shoulders to cry on. Neighbors and community members bring us food and encourage us to eat if we are in too much anguish to register hunger. Our workplaces offer us time off to grieve and receive the support we need and many also offer counseling services to aid our recovery.

However, when our heartbreak is caused by a romantic breakup or by the loss of a beloved pet—which are not considered sanctioned forms of grief—our support systems are likely to respond very differently. As we shall see, this lack of support impacts us in significant ways. Not only are we robbed of an essential curative ingredient, we are often faced with additional stresses that compound our suffering, increase our emotional distress, and complicate our recovery.

What makes this lack of support even more impactful is that we don't exactly have a quiver full of therapeutic arrows to deploy when our heart is broken. We have been experiencing broken hearts for millennia and yet most of us know of only two healing agents: social support and time. Losing the former leaves us with only time as a remedy, a variable over which we have no control whatsoever, which is why heartbreak often makes us feel so helpless. This is also why so few of us seek the counsel of a therapist when our heart gets broken. We assume the only significant thing a therapist could offer in such situations is support, and most of us hope to receive that from our friends and loved ones, at least initially.

Therefore, it should not be surprising that the vast majority of my heartbroken patients came to therapy to discuss other issues entirely (dating and relationships often among them) and their heart happened to get broken during treatment. The patients we will meet in the coming chapters represent a variety of heart-breaks and circumstances. Their stories reflect the various ways we are impacted when our heart gets broken, the mistakes we make that set us back, the roles our support networks play, and the different roads we can take to recovery.

Heartbreak is painful enough when there are signs of its impending arrival, when it comes upon us slowly. But when it assaults us suddenly and unexpectedly, it can be as shocking as it is devastating. Therefore, when I see heartbreak coming from miles away, I always sound a warning. Some of my patients heed these warnings, many do not. Such is the lure of hope and need when infatuation teases our heart with the promise of deeper love. And then every once in a while, I am as blindsided by the heartbreak that befalls my patients as they are.

•   •   •

Kathy was in her late twenties when she first began psychotherapy for issues that had nothing to do with heartbreak. Raised in a small town in the Midwest, she had moved to New York for graduate school, fell in love with the city, and decided to stay. An excellent student, she had no trouble landing a corporate position as soon as she graduated. When I met Kathy for our first session she was well-groomed and well-dressed in a crisp pantsuit and heels. With poise and confidence that matched her firm handshake, she sat forward on the couch, legs folded and hands on her lap, showing no signs of nervousness about having to tell a complete stranger her life story, or highlights thereof.

I was still settling into my seat when she smiled and said in a rich, smooth voice, "Shall I tell you why I'm here?" Kathy's body language conveyed patience and self-control yet she was clearly eager to get down to business.

"Please do," I said with a smile.

Kathy took a deep breath and began "I was that girl who plans her entire life in middle school, wedding scrapbook and all." She ticked the steps off on her fingers. "I'd go to college then graduate school, land a good job, and start dating my future husband by age twenty-seven, twenty-eight at the latest. We'd move in

together after a year, get engaged a year after that, and marry before I was thirty." The obvious distress on Kathy's face told me her life had not gone as planned.

"I did college, finished graduate school, and got a good job," she continued. "But when it came time to find my future husband, what I found instead was a lump in my breast."

Given her youth and excellent overall health, Kathy's doctors suggested she get the strongest chemotherapy possible and Kathy agreed.

"They told me the side effects would be bad," Kathy went on, "and they were. I could deal with the hair loss, the terrible nausea, the sores in my mouth, but I had intense nerve pain all over my body." Kathy shuddered at the recollection. "It was excruciating." She took a breath and composed herself before continuing. "My friends and family were amazing. They totally got me through it."

Fortunately, Kathy's chemotherapy was successful. Eager to get back to her life plan, she turned her efforts toward recovering. She ate healthy foods and worked out as much as her stamina allowed. Her body slowly regained strength, her hair grew back, and she eventually felt ready to venture back into the dating world. Over the course of her treatment and recovery, many of Kathy's friends had gotten engaged and she found herself attending bachelorette parties or weddings almost every month. Tired of attending them alone, she decided to take action.

"I sent my friends a group text with two words: *I'm ready!*" Kathy said, smiling. "Within days I had blind dates coming at me from every direction. I literally caught myself walking around humming 'It's raining men.' My life was finally getting back on track. I felt happy for the first time in almost two years."

Kathy sighed heavily and her eyes welled with tears. "And then, last month I found a lump in my other breast." She dabbed at her eyes as her tears fell. "That's why I'm here. The thought of having to do it all over again is just ... horrible ... I'm going to need help getting through it."

Kathy had already endured more than most and now she would have to endure even more. That someone so young had to go through so much seemed truly unfair. What heartened me was Kathy's incredible emotional strength. Despite facing her second battle with cancer in two years, she had not lost hope or stopped fighting. Indeed, her response was both wise and psychologically healthy—she was reaching out to a therapist to shore up her support system in anticipation of the struggle ahead.

For the next year, I witnessed Kathy fight cancer with determination, dignity, and strength. The side effects of the second chemotherapy were just as challenging as the first but she never considered stopping the treatment. She simply set her sights on the goalpost of remission and never wavered.

I was thrilled to learn that Kathy's resolve had again paid off, as her second treatment was also effective and she was once again in remission. This time it took her body longer to recover but eventually she got stronger, her hair grew back, her scars healed, and the day again came when she sent an *I'm ready!* text to her wonderful circle of supportive friends.

"And it began 'raining men' again," Kathy said in our session.

"Hallelujah!" I responded, quoting the next line of the song.

A few months later, Kathy met Rich, a stock analyst in his midthirties, and fell in love. Rich seemed to be exactly the kind of man Kathy needed: gentle, considerate, and affirming. He complemented her, he kissed her scars and let her know how attracted he was to her, and he took her to romantic restaurants and on spontaneous weekend getaways to the beach. Kathy had never been happier.

Six months after they started dating Kathy came into my office beaming. "Good news!"

I tried to hide my excitement. Rich had just taken Kathy to a romantic bed and breakfast in New England. It was fall and the foliage was at its peak—it was the perfect time and place for a proposal. "Yes?" I asked as casually as I could.

Kathy took a deep breath and announced, "I started a Pinterest page!"

"That's . . . great!" I said, forcing a smile.

"Oh! You thought . . . but that's actually the point. He didn't ask me yet but after the great weekend we had, it feels like he will any day now. So I went to my parents' house and got my old wedding scrapbook. I scanned it in and started a wedding Pinterest page!"

This time my smile was authentic.

Two weeks later, Rich nervously asked Kathy to dinner in their favorite spot—a quiet romantic restaurant with private booths and low lighting. After their drinks arrived, he took her hand—and broke up with her.

Rich explained that although he cared about Kathy tremendously and loved spending time with her, his feelings simply hadn't progressed the way hers had. Since he felt sure she was not "the one," he thought it was only fair to let her know.

Kathy was devastated. Once again, her friends and family rallied around her in her hour of need. And her need was great. I thought I had seen Kathy at her most despondent but her anguish was profound. She cried for weeks, she barely functioned at work, and she spent hours sitting in the dark, paralyzed by emotional pain. She frequently missed sessions and despite my urging, was unable to get herself to therapy more than once a month.

The breakup was all Kathy could talk about, both with me and with her friends. But while my sessions with her were few and far between, Kathy's friends racked up countless hours providing support, solace, and advice. After several months, they began exhibiting signs of impatience with Kathy's inability to move on. By the time I saw Kathy a month later, their impatience had turned to obvious frustration.

Saddened as I was to hear about her friends losing patience, I was not surprised. I had seen this happen countless times. When our heart is broken, what determines others' compassion is not how much emotional pain we *actually* feel but how much emotional pain they believe we *should* feel. Kathy had exceeded her friends' unspoken statute of limitations for mourning the relationship and their empathy and support were rapidly evaporating as a result. In its place Kathy was met with impatience, irritability, and even resentment.

Before we judge Kathy's friends too harshly, it is important to consider that many of us have probably been guilty of similar judgments when our friends' or loved ones' broken hearts took longer to mend than our subjective standards allotted, whether we expressed our impatience with them or not. Being around someone we care about when they are in sharp pain of any kind is a fundamentally distressing experience. In order to provide them with support and compassion we have to first contain these unpleasant feelings within ourselves (or we will be too preoccupied with our own emotional reactions to focus on theirs). We do so with the tacit assumption that the efforts required to tolerate our own distress in order to be there for them will be met by commensurate efforts on their part to heal and move on. When we see their recovery stall, we assume (unconsciously) that they failed to live up to their part of the bargain and so we feel less compelled to live up to ours. Thus our empathy fades and resentment rears its head.

Unfortunately, our friends and loved ones are not the only people who can lose patience and compassion when our recovery stalls. One of the damaging ripple effects of losing social support is that we often internalize the impatience of those around us and lose *self*-compassion as well. We are then left with the double whammy of a massive reduction in social support and a massive increase in self-criticism.

"My friends are right," Kathy sighed in that same session. "I should have moved on months ago but I can't, not without knowing why this happened. I still love him! I still miss him. I wish I didn't . . . but I just do!"

Kathy had been through two extremely harsh cancer treatments and never lost hope or motivation. In fact, she had displayed incredible emotional strength throughout the four years of her medical ordeal. But something was preventing her from marshaling her considerable internal strength and determination in order to heal her broken heart. And now, after losing her friends' support, I worried her recovery might stall completely.

One thing Kathy said made me curious: "not without knowing why this happened." After all, Rich had explained his reasons for breaking up—he cared for her deeply but he simply wasn't in love. Apparently, Kathy had rejected his explanation (despite how reasonable it was), had become convinced there was something he was not telling her, and obsessed with figuring out what it was. I asked her whether she discussed this issue with her friends.

"That's pretty much all I discuss with them," she responded.

I now began to understand why her friends had lost patience. Creating mysteries and conspiracies where none exist is a common response to romantic breakups. Our mind unconsciously assumes that if the emotional pain we feel is so dramatic, it must have an equally dramatic cause, even when it does not. Her friends probably took Rich's explanation at face value and therefore perceived Kathy's insistence on finding alternative explanations as an unnecessary wild goose chase. In other words, they probably felt that by rejecting Rich's reasons for the breakup and pursuing alternate explanations she was preventing herself from moving on, and it was that which caused them to lose empathy and compassion.

Indeed, one of the biggest mistakes we tend to make when our heart gets broken is we overtax our support systems by voicing aloud all our internal ruminations about what went wrong. Doing so in the initial aftermath of a breakup is understandable. But when we keep repeating the same questions over and over for weeks and months at a time—"Why wasn't I good enough?" "What went wrong?" "Why did they lie to me?" "Why did they stop loving me?"—while reaching no new insights and without acknowledging those that have already been reached, even our strongest supporters can become frustrated.

Therefore, despite how much we may be hurting, we have to keep our eye on whether we are overburdening our support systems and making efforts to provide "breaks" for those doing the lion's share of emotional support. To be clear, I am not advocating that we forgo the emotional validation and compassion we still need. As I explained to Kathy when she told me about her friends losing compassion, "You can still get support from them but in a different way. After all, they still love you and care for you, even if their patience seems thin at the moment. I'm pretty sure that if you talk about other things for a short while, they will still know you're hurting and they will demonstrate their caring with a hug, a look, or a squeeze of the hand. You just have to be open to accepting their support in the ways they are currently able to give it."

As we shall see later on, Kathy heard my concerns and understood them, and she even made changes that allowed the tensions with her friends to ease. However, she still could not accept Rich's explanation for the breakup and she still felt a powerful drive to unravel his "true" reasons. Still heartbroken and feeling more alone than she had previously, she truly missed the unequivocal support her friends had provided. Our support networks play a significant role in our recovery from a broken heart. As such, their absence can be just as damaging when our heartbreak is due to the death of a beloved pet.

## Losing Best Friends and Longtime Companions

Ben was a writer for a large corporation who came to see me in his midforties after both his parents had died within six months of each other. Ben had divorced in his late thirties, had no children, and a limited number of friends. His parents were the only family Ben had left and he struggled after their death. He had difficulty completing assignments on time and felt himself slipping into a depression. A human resources manager at his company intervened and suggested Ben consider psychotherapy. He came to see me soon thereafter.

I worked with Ben for a few months. He took therapy seriously and was able to move through the roughest stages of the grieving process and get to a better place emotionally. It was at that point he decided to take a break from therapy.

Given that both his mood and his functioning at work had improved, I supported his decision. Ben promised to be in touch if he felt the need and I reassured him he could contact me whenever he wanted.

Seven years passed. Then one bright spring morning, I received an e-mail from him:

*I need to see you again but you're going to think it's silly because it's about Bover. I know it's ridiculous to go to therapy to talk about a dog but he's really sick and I need to talk about it. I know it sounds stupid and I feel embarrassed to ask but please let me know if it's okay to make an appointment ASAP.*

My heart pinched as I read Ben's words. I remembered both him and Bover well. Ben worked from home and was alone in his apartment all day, so he had decided to get a dog for companionship soon after his divorce. He adopted a rescue pup he named Bover, an adorable Labrador and golden retriever mix. Bover was Ben's first dog and he was totally smitten with him from day one. He devoted hours to playing with his new puppy and training him to do simple tricks. He proudly walked him around the neighborhood and Bover, who was a ham even by dog standards, accrued fans and admirers everywhere. Even people who knew Ben previously began referring to him as "Bover's dad."

When Ben's parents first got sick, Ben took Bover with him whenever he visited them, just to be able to have Bover with him on the drive back and forth. When they were hospitalized he asked their neighbors to watch Bover while he spent hours at their bedside. Ben also received support from his boss, who was considerate and understanding. He gave Ben time off to care for his parents as their conditions worsened and to grieve them when they died.

I would like to think therapy was the vital ingredient that helped Ben get through his parents' death but it was not. What truly kept him going during that dark period was Bover.

"He sleeps with me in the bed at night," Ben told me in our first session. "He sits by me when I work. Yesterday, I was watching TV and thinking about my dad, and I guess I started to cry. I didn't even notice I had tears on my cheek until Bover came over and began licking my hand. I swear he can tell when I'm sad. He's the most amazing dog!"

Bover was. Ben would often bring him to our sessions, where he would lie at the foot of the couch, his head resting on Ben's foot. Truly attuned to Ben's mood and emotional distress, when Ben teared up or cried, Bover would sit up and lick his hand or rest his head on Ben's knee. The bond between them was powerful and undeniable. With Bover's health failing, I could only imagine how distraught Ben must be.

I met with Ben the next day. He came alone. Almost fifteen years old now, Bover was deaf and almost entirely blind, and he often became anxious and restless in unfamiliar places. Since I had moved offices since I last saw Ben, he thought it best to leave Bover at home. Ben was extremely upset during our session and I comforted him as best I could. We set up another time to meet the following week.

But Bover's health deteriorated rapidly and Ben had to take him to the vet the next day. Bover rallied at first but then declined again a few days later. The vet determined he required surgery. Ben had already used his personal days and most of his vacation days to care for Bover over multiple health emergencies and vet visits. He used his last vacation day to stay by Bover's side as he recovered at home after the surgery. The next morning, Bover slipped into a coma.

Out of both personal and vacation days, Ben called in sick to work so he could rush Bover back to the vet. His boss called him on his cell phone a few hours later after Ben didn't answer his landline. Ben admitted he was at the veterinary hospital and explained that his dog was very sick. His boss was furious. He insisted Ben get back to work immediately so he could meet an important deadline.

Ben had no choice. He left Bover at the veterinary hospital and went home to finish his work. That afternoon, the vet called. Bover was failing rapidly. Ignoring the consequences of leaving his assignment incomplete, Ben rushed to his dog's side. When he arrived at the vet's, Bover was unconscious and breathing shallowly. Ben reached over and softly stroked his dog's head, tears streaking down his cheeks.

"And then something amazing happened," Ben told me when we met the following evening. "Bover's eyes never opened when I touched him. So I put my hand near his nose so he could smell that it was me and . . . he licked my hand." Ben collapsed into sobs. "He knew I was crying and he licked my hand, just like he always did. He licked my hand! And then he died."

Although I often feel deeply sad when working with a patient whose heart is broken, I am rarely moved to tears. But Ben's description of Bover's last moments had me lunging for the tissue box. The enormity of Ben's loss was apparent. Bover's faithful companionship had eased Ben's loneliness after his divorce, his loyal devotion had comforted Ben when his parents died, and his playful and exuberant presence had been Ben's emotional anchor for the past fifteen years. Ben's heart was absolutely shattered.

But he was given no time to grieve.

His boss called Ben into the office the next morning and put him on official warning for absenteeism. When Ben tried to explain what Bover had meant to him, his boss rolled his eyes and exclaimed, "It's just an animal! Get over it!" Ben tried to negotiate and asked to take a few days off without pay. His boss exploded. "Grow up, Ben! My six-year-old had to flush her goldfish down the toilet last week. You think *she* got a week off school to cry in the dark?"

Fortunately, I was able to intervene and write Ben a medical note that excused him from work for a couple of days. Ben's human resources department had no choice but to accept my note but his boss openly voiced his disapproval. Upon his return he assigned Ben a heavier than normal workload with ruthless deadlines. The threat of losing his job looming over him, Ben had no choice but to work through his tears.

His inexcusable lack of compassion notwithstanding, Ben's boss is by no means an aberration. Our institutions rarely recognize how significant and traumatic it can be to lose a cherished pet and they rarely afford those who experience such loss the compassion and understanding they desperately need. This lack of recognition makes an already painful grieving process even more difficult and complicated than it otherwise would be.

To be clear, individuals (bosses as well) often respond with empathy and understanding to those whose heart is broken by romantic love or the death of a beloved pet. It is society as a whole that ignores the severity of emotional pain such losses evoke and the profound impact they have on our functioning. Expecting Ben to be productive at work when his dog is dying in the animal hospital is naïve bordering on foolish. Ben's boss forced him to sit at his desk but he was there in body only. His mind was with Bover.

What is even more unfortunate is that too many of us internalize these kinds of insensitive, ignorant, and uninformed expectations and judge ourselves by them, despite how profoundly they contradict our emotional experience. Ben's initial e-mail to me is a good illustration of this contradiction. Its tone was extremely tentative and apologetic, not only because Ben was worried I would consider his emotional distress illegitimate but because he himself felt embarrassed by it. Adding layers of embarrassment or shame to the intense emotional distress we feel when our pet dies only exacerbates our heartache and complicates our recovery.

This was why I allowed myself to display how sad I was when Ben told me about Bover dying. It was important for him to see me shedding a tear—something I had never done when his parents died—so I could validate how natural and legitimate it was for him to feel so heartbroken. In order to balance the total dismissiveness with which Ben's boss continued to treat his grief, I made sure to allow my feelings of empathy and compassion to register clearly on my face and in my voice as the weeks progressed.

It took many months for Ben to recover from Bover's death, far longer than it had taken him to recover when his parents died. In part, this was because Ben's parents had not been an integral part of his daily life. They were not strongly associated with the many experiences and situations that comprised Ben's personal and social activities whereas Bover was. In addition, there was no doubt in my mind that Ben's inability to express his grief at work and the total lack of compassion his boss demonstrated for his emotional pain made his recovery significantly more challenging.

When our heart is broken and our institutions deny us the support and understanding we deserve, it is important for us to reject their dismissive message and actively seek to have our feelings validated elsewhere in whatever way we can. There are more options to do so than we realize. Since Ben had no family and so few friends, I tried to fill that void as best I could over the months that followed. I also suggested Ben join a support group for people who have lost pets. The fact that such groups are sprouting up all over is yet another indication of the lack of societal recognition people who lose their pets are afforded. I encouraged Ben to reach out to a man he knew from a dog run he visited with Bover who had recently lost his dog as well.

Bover had been Ben's loyal friend for fifteen years and he was associated with every facet of Ben's life. Generally speaking, when our heart is broken, the more substantial our relationship and our connection are (whether with a pet or the object of our romantic affections), the deeper our grief is likely to be and the longer it might take us to recover. What makes heartbreak so different from other forms of grief is that sometimes even the loss of a brief and superficial connection can pierce our core to the depths.

### The Dating Minefield Is Littered with Broken Hearts

Lauren, the twenty-seven-year-old daughter of an actuary and an engineer, came to therapy to work on her cripplingly low self-esteem and significant social anxiety. A medical student who was far more comfortable with thought and logic than with emotions (hers and others'), she usually preferred the company of textbooks and petri dishes to that of people. Her sexual experience amounted to little more than a few alcohol-infused make-out sessions in college and her current dating life was nonexistent.

As is the case with many who suffer from social anxiety, years of fear and avoidance had warped some of her perceptions and fostered highly self-critical and overly pessimistic beliefs about both her worth and her chances of success in the dating world. As is the case with many who have very low self-esteem, she perceived herself to be significantly less attractive (both physically and personality-wise) than she actually was. Our initial work consisted of me enlisting Lauren's penchant for reason to challenge some of her distorted assumptions about her looks and her social desirability in order to create a more conducive mind-set for working on her self-esteem.

A few months into therapy, Lauren had made enough progress that a friend was finally able to persuade her to join a popular dating site. A week later, Lauren announced she had just scheduled her first date since college. "My friend has been swiping left and right for years," she said. "She told me it's typical to have more bad first dates than good. So I guess the key is to try to have fun but keep my hopes moderate."

I was glad to hear Lauren was keeping her expectations low. She had not been on a formal date in years and her "dating skills" were likely to be rusty at best. I suggested she think of her first few dates as "practice," with the goal of getting more comfortable with the dating scene. If something comes of them, great, but it might take her a bit to get the swing of things. Rejection and disappointment are such an inherent part of the dating experience that by reinforcing Lauren's moderate expectations I hoped they would not impact her as severely as they might otherwise.

The next day Lauren left me an excited message, eager to share how much she had enjoyed her date. Apparently, she and her date had several drinks and talked for over three hours. She was absolutely thrilled.

Our next session was two days later. Lauren never showed up. She left me a message that night, apologizing and explaining she was too distraught to come to therapy. I found out what happened only later: Lauren hadn't heard from her date for

two days, so she texted him and expressed interest in seeing
him again. When he responded several hours later, he sent her
a terse text saying he had enjoyed the date as well but wasn't
interested in seeing her again.

"I literally spent three days crying in bed," Lauren explained
when we met next, the hurt still apparent on her face. "I missed
school and my rotations, it was terrible. I was a mess! The only
thing worse than how broken I felt was how humiliated I felt
about feeling so broken. Everyone warned me to be cautious
and keep my hopes in check and I did. I really did! I went to the
date expecting so little. And then I fell to pieces anyway. What's
wrong with me? Why did I feel so heartbroken after only one
date?"

We tend to associate romantic heartbreak with substantial
and meaningful loss. So why did Lauren feel so heartbroken
after a single date? And why did the apex of the emotional pain
she felt last for three whole days when her expectations had
been so moderate to begin with?

The answer to the first question involves a common mistake
many of us make when we enter or reenter the dating world.
Lauren knew it was important to keep her hopes moderate and
protect her self-esteem and she was careful to set low expectations *before* she went on her date, but she neglected to keep
her expectations low *after* it. Once the date went well, Lauren's
expectations quickly soared, setting her up for a much bigger
blow.

As to the second question, what kept Lauren housebound
for three full days was not the initial blow of rejection but the

shame and isolation that came thereafter. She was so convinced her friends (and me) would consider her heartbreak to be ridiculous and inappropriate that she was afraid to reach out to the very people who could have provided her comfort and support. Her self-imposed isolation, the ridicule she imagined facing when she told her friends how devastated she felt, and the ensuing lack of emotional validation, support, and empathy significantly prolonged her suffering.

Lauren is by no means an anomaly. I have worked with scores of people whose hearts got broken after a single date, something which is especially common for those who reenter the dating world after not having been in it for a long period of time (whether they were single or in long-term relationships). While this kind of heartbreak is usually short lived, it can be incredibly intense and painful nonetheless. Unfortunately, in almost every case, they felt the very same shame and embarrassment Lauren did, and having those feelings significantly added to the emotional pain and distress they felt and made them extremely hesitant to set up any other dates.

That certain types of heartbreak are disenfranchised in society makes healing a broken heart difficult enough, we certainly should not add to the injustice by disenfranchising our own emotional pain. The worst thing we could do for ourselves when we are hurting is to internalize these arbitrary standards, become self-critical as a result, and deny ourselves the very empathy and support we so badly need.

· · ·

Kathy's heart was broken when the man she dated for six months and expected to marry broke up with her, Ben's heartbreak was a result of losing a beloved pet that had been a hugely significant part of his life for fifteen years, and Lauren had her heart broken after a single date. While they each faced separate hurdles on their road to recovery, one hurdle they should not have had to deal with was the withdrawal or absence of support and validation from the people and institutions around them.

There is a reason most cultures have mourning rituals that involve the larger community. When we are grieving, we need empathy, we need compassion, we need hugs. Grief researchers have long acknowledged that heartbreak is a form of grief. Our communities, our societies, and many of the people in them do not. Until, of course, they are the ones who are heartbroken.

But why do we consider heartbreak so unworthy of the same concern and respect as other forms of grief?

One of the main reasons society trivializes certain types of heartbreak is that we do not fully comprehend the extent to which our mind, our body, and especially our brain are impacted when our heart is broken. But now, after decades of study, scientists know much more than we used to about the phenomenon of heartbreak. The findings of the studies we'll explore in the pages to come have taken much of the mystery out of the unconscious and unseen processes that take place in our brain and body when our heart is broken. Understanding exactly what happens to us when we are heartbroken is an essential step in being able to heal and move on.

# 2 When Hearts Break, Brains and Bodies Break Too

Heartbreak is a hijacker. The emotional anguish it causes invades our thoughts, captures our attention, seizes our focus, and dominates our awareness. Like a black hole that pulls everything toward it, all we see and do is now experienced in reference to our broken heart, viewed through the lens of our loss. The emotional pain is so inescapable and the tightness in our chest so real, it feels as though our heart is literally broken. This metaphor of a "broken heart," combined with the fact that it was caused by a single loss, makes us perceive heartbreak as a discrete and specific injury—as if there is one simple thing wrong with us. But heartbreak is neither a simple injury nor a *specific* one—it is *systemic* and complex. Heartbreak impacts far more than our mind and emotions. It affects our body, our brain, our functioning, and our relationships and it does so in far-reaching and surprising ways.

Our oversimplified view of heartbreak is more consequential than we realize. Because we lack a clear understanding of what exactly gets "broken" (other than our metaphorical heart) we are likely to misunderstand, misinterpret, or downright ignore the many aspects of our mental and behavioral functioning that are influenced by our broken hearts. As a result, our recovery from heartbreak can take longer and it can be less complete. Further, we are likely to be less empathetic and compassionate toward our loved ones when it is their heart that gets broken. And of course, it also contributes to the unfortunate societal disenfranchisement of heartbreak.

In order to heal as thoroughly and as rapidly as we can, we must first gain a more accurate appreciation of what heartbreak actually does to us. And the best place to start is at the literal top—our brain.

A few years ago, Ethan Kross and his colleagues at the University of Michigan put out a call for people who had been through a recent and painful romantic breakup. One by one, these paid volunteers were placed in fMRI machines (scanners that reveal areas of the brain with increased blood flow, suggesting increased activity) and instructed to stare at a photograph of the person who broke their heart and relive the breakup in their mind as the scanner gathered images of their brain, one razor-thin slice at a time.

Rough as that might sound the volunteers' ordeal was not over yet. The researchers wanted to be able to compare what happens in our brain when we experience sharp *emotional* pain to what happens when we experience sharp *physical* pain. And so back into the fMRI machine the volunteers went. This time, a Neurosensory Analyzer (a machine that transfers heat to the skin of the forearm) was used to apply increasing levels of uncomfortable heat to the volunteers' forearm for seven-second intervals. At first the heat was set to arouse only mild discomfort. But it went up from there, peaking at pain levels subjects rated an eight on a ten-point scale, where ten was "unbearable."

When the scientists compared the two brain scans, what they saw was remarkable. The exact same areas of the brain became

activated when subjects relived their heartbreak as when they experienced the highest degree of physical pain—the level that was only a couple of notches below "unbearable."

To put these findings in context, think back to when you had a really bad headache, stomachache, or backache. Few of us would consider the discomfort such aches cause as being anywhere near "unbearable," yet we typically find them quite debilitating nonetheless. Most of us find it difficult to work efficiently, study productively, or complete certain tasks in such situations, and we often find it necessary to lie down or take over-the-counter medication in order to resume our normal activities.

Now imagine trying to do your job, study, or complete your responsibilities if the pain you were experiencing was near "unbearable" levels. Imagine trying to think clearly or creatively, reason, problem-solve, attend to small details, operate heavy machinery, or even compose a lengthy e-mail. Further, consider that the subjects in these experiments were exposed to near "unbearable" pain for only a few seconds. A broken heart can cause sharp emotional pain that lasts for hours, days, weeks, even months.

The fMRI experiment was only one of dozens of similar studies, all of which demonstrated how heartbreak elicits reactions in our brains and bodies that cause substantial cognitive and functional impairments. In one study, the mere thought of being without a significant other was enough to temporarily lower participants' IQ (their intelligence quotient) and significantly harm their performance on tasks involving logic and reasoning.

Now it is easier to understand why Kathy, the cancer survivor who had trouble getting over her six-month relationship with Rich, failed to register Rich's rationale for breaking up as reasonable and began seeking alternative explanations. It is also clearer why Ben struggled to function at work after his dog Bover died.

Indeed, this is what makes having a broken heart so devastating. Not only are we in severe emotional anguish and not only are the effects of our anguish severely debilitating, but too often, both our pain and our *functional impairment* go unacknowledged and ignored. We would never expect someone to function normally at school or their job if they were experiencing near "unbearable" physical pain throughout the day. But Ben was given no consideration for his profound emotional suffering or for its debilitating impact on his functioning.

Registering severe physical pain is only one of the ways our brain reacts when our heart is broken. There is another and it is much more insidious.

### You're Gonna Have to Face It You're Addicted to Love

One of the main reasons Kathy rejected Rich's explanation for why he broke up with her was that it came only two weeks after their weekend in New England. Kathy became convinced something must have happened that weekend to tilt the relationship off course (even though at the time she thought it had gone very well). She spent months combing through her memories of that weekend, repeatedly examining every photograph and selfie she had taken and every text she had sent and received during and after those three days. She was utterly obsessed.

The question was: Why didn't she just accept Rich's explanation and move on? Surely it would have been less painful to do so than to go through anguish for months at a time. Why was she so compelled to go on this wild goose chase?

Reliving old memories and going through pictures is something many of us might do in the first hours, days, or even weeks following a breakup (or the loss of a beloved pet). However, our urge to do so usually declines over time and at some point ceases altogether. Kathy's did not, despite the fact that the exercise must have been extremely painful. After all, she was submerging herself in memories of a happy and romantic weekend for minutes and hours at a time, only to then return to the harsh reality of the breakup.

"I feel like a detective searching through a crime scene," Kathy explained in one of our rare sessions during this period. "I know the clues are there but I just can't put them together!"

Kathy might have felt like a detective but her metaphor was totally incorrect. She wasn't behaving like Sherlock Holmes—she was behaving like a drug addict.

Studies of the brain have revealed that romantic love involves the activation of both brain structures (such as the ventral tegmental area, the caudate nuclei, and the nucleus accumbens) and neurochemistry that are highly associated with addiction.

Indeed, when our heart is broken by romantic love or infatuation, our brain responds very similarly to the brains of addicts going through withdrawal from cocaine or heroin. We become intensely focused on the person who broke our heart (the "drug") and feel intense cravings for them that are extremely difficult to banish, ignore, or soothe. The lack of contact with the person (i.e., not getting our fix) makes us unable to focus, disturbs our sleep and appetite, causes anxiety, lethargy, irritability, crying spells, depression, and intense feelings of need (loneliness) that no one but our heartbreaker can ease—just like cocaine and heroin do.

Kathy was experiencing powerful symptoms of "withdrawal" from Rich but she was not aware of it. Her cravings for him (and for the relationship) were so strong, she was getting her "fix" the way she could—in her mind. If Kathy couldn't have the real "heroin" of being with Rich, she could at least get the "methadone" of the memories of the time she shared with him.

Since Kathy was unaware of how her brain was driving her behavior, she made sense of her intense ruminating the only way she could, by convincing herself there was a mystery to be solved. But the real reason she kept revisiting that weekend was not because something had gone wrong but the opposite—because of how great the weekend had been. By replaying these happy moments as vividly as she could (albeit under the guise of a search for "clues"), she was giving herself "fixes," small tastes of what she craved so badly—the feeling of being with Rich.

This "fix-seeking" addict-like behavior is very common when our heart is broken and we can be quite sophisticated in the justifications we concoct to engage in contact with the person we crave (whether face-to-face, electronically, or in our mind). I once worked with a woman whose ex-boyfriend kept "remembering" stuff he had left at her apartment that he needed to pick up. He knew she did not have a doorman and would therefore have to meet him in person for each handoff. First he asked for a T-shirt he had left in her drawer. A few days later it was gym shorts. My patient drew the line when he asked to retrieve a chipped dessert dish he had forgotten in her kitchen cupboard.

Of course, many of us skip justifications altogether and simply indulge these powerful urges, unaware we are doing so in order to get our "fix" and keep our symptoms of withdrawal at bay. We might send dozens of texts, call to hear their voice on their outgoing message, "accidently" include them on group e-mails, hang out where we hope to run into them, seek out their friends and family, or "mistakenly" dial them on our phones. But in the era of social media, the most common way people satisfy their craving for the person who broke their heart is to stalk them digitally.

## Cyberstalking from the Comfort of Our Phones

Dev, a divorced sales manager in his forties, had initially come to therapy to focus on issues related to his professional career. A few sessions into our work, he casually mentioned that after having a bad fight with his current girlfriend, he stayed up all night looking through his old college girlfriend's Facebook, Instagram, Twitter, and Snapchat feeds.

"No, no, it's cool," he assured me after my eyebrows shot up before I could stop them. "I'm totally over her. It's just something I do when I'm stressed," he said, waving his hand dismissively. "I use accounts with a fake name so it's totally harmless. She doesn't know it's me."

It had been more than twenty years since Dev's college girlfriend broke up with him. He had been in an eleven-year marriage and a couple of short-term relationships since then. I asked him when he began cyberstalking his college ex.

"I guess when I was married," Dev admitted. "I usually did it after my ex-wife and I argued. You know, to calm down."

According to Dev, he would go for months without his college girlfriend even crossing his mind. But every so often, he found himself compelled to obsessively review her social media activity. When I characterized his behavior in these terms, Dev objected. He didn't see himself as *compelled* nor did he perceive his behavior as *obsessive*. "It's just a distraction," he insisted, "like Candy Crush—it's just a silly way to let off steam."

"You stayed up all night," I pointed out. "That's a lot of steam. Did you make it to work the next day?" Dev shook his head. "And here we've been discussing how much your career means to you," I continued. "Can we agree that if you stayed up all night and risked missing work, the urge to do so must have been pretty powerful?" This time Dev nodded.

Dev's behavior reminded me of what often happens when people stop using addictive substances. An ex-smoker who had not touched a cigarette in years or even decades, might, in response to a stressful situation or trigger, feel a sudden intense

need for a cigarette. Alcoholics and former substance abusers might have similar unexpected moments of powerful cravings, even years into their sobriety.

Most former addicts (smokers included) are able to manage such pangs because they are highly aware of how risky it would be to indulge them. One drag of a cigarette can reactivate days of intense cravings for nicotine for an ex-smoker. A single dose of heroin can have a similar effect on an opioid addict. But few of us are aware that indulging the urge to look up the person who broke our heart years ago can reactivate our "addiction" to them. We see our actions as being motivated by mere curiosity and the outcome of our efforts as essentially harmless. We are also likely to ignore the fact that these kinds of cyber searches are almost always responses to psychological stressors such as setbacks, loneliness, or frustration in our current relationship. That such behaviors are related to addiction responses is the last thing we would consider.

The impulse notwithstanding, what makes cyberstalking so common is the current ease with which we can satisfy these romantic cravings (even if we don't recognize them as such). No matter where we are or what the hour, our phones are always there, ready to teleport us across time and space to become hidden observers of another person's life. Google searches, personal blogs, social media, and other platforms can provide highly personal and even intimate information in the form of text, pictures, videos, and soon full 3-D immersion, creating moments of "pseudo-connection" that can feel almost as real and substantive as having actual contact.

Much as drug addicts are urged to erase the contact information of their dealers from their electronic devices, when we find ourselves cyberstalking someone repeatedly, we have to realize we are playing with an old wound (or a fresh one, as cyberstalking is something that happens much more frequently in the early stages of a breakup). If we want to avoid deepening the pain we feel about a fresh loss or reactivating the wounds of an old one, we have to eliminate our options to do so and go on a blocking and deleting spree. Difficult as it is to unfriend, unfollow, block or delete our access to the person's cyber world, it is the only prudent way to prevent ourselves from stalking them again in the future.

Of course, as any cyberstalker knows, eliminating direct access to our ex is entirely insufficient, as we will then be tempted to spend even more time scanning the social media accounts of their friends and family in hopes of finding news and images of them in their feeds. Therefore, we have to truly erase all access points. It might feel overly harsh, final, and even brutal to burn all our cyber bridges to our ex's life but if we are serious about ceasing our cyberstalking and easing our emotional attachment to them, we simply must do it.

Because cyberstalking usually happens when breakups are fresh and since Dev's breakup with his college girlfriend happened so many years in the past, I was curious to hear how the relationship had ended.

"It was rough," Dev responded. "She was my first . . . everything. She decided to move back to California after graduation and didn't want a long-distance relationship. I tried to convince her to give it a try at least, but no dice. I really loved her . . . you know how it is . . . you have no pride. So, I totally begged. I begged her to stay then I begged her to give the long-distance thing a chance. But her mind was made up. Like I said, no pride, so I kept at it regardless. But the more I begged the colder she became. I ended up getting really pissed. I told her she would never find anyone as good as me, that she would never be happy in California. She refused to talk to me after that."

Dev looked down as he continued. "I didn't want to accept it was over. I took it hard man, real hard. I was like a crazy person—screaming and yelling one minute and crying like a baby the next."

Dev's experience was dramatic yet typical. Many of us struggle to accept the reality of a breakup when our heart is broken. Known as the *protest phase*, we are likely to try anything and everything to win back the affection of the person we love, even when they are exceedingly clear that the relationship is over. Dev tried reasoning and convincing, guilt trips, and even begging, but all to no avail.

When we do finally recognize we cannot salvage the relationship, another common reaction is often triggered: *abandonment rage*, which is characterized by quickly vacillating between utter fury and total devastation. In the days following the breakup, Dev left his ex-girlfriend dozens of phone messages—long angry tirades, then tearful apologies, then another round of furious expletives.

Coming to terms with the reality of a breakup is often different from the psychological process we go through when dealing with other forms of grief. We do not necessarily move through a linear progression of the five stages of grief (from shock or denial, to anger and rage, bargaining, despair, and finally acceptance). Instead, we often vacillate between denial and despair, hope and rage, helplessness and fury. It is these emotional swings that made Dev feel like a "crazy person." Indeed, the arc of our emotional pendulum can feel so uncharacteristically wide in such situations, many whose heart is broken actually fear they are "going crazy" or heading toward a full-fledged mental breakdown.

Although heartbreak can cause some people to have a real mental breakdown, the vast majority of us do not decompensate to that extent. While we might have moments in which we act "out of our minds" and do things we ordinarily would not, these are usually just "moments" or "incidents" after which we regain our reason and mental faculties. Episodes of anxiety and depression are also very common when our heart is broken, as are disturbances in sleep, appetite, or impulsivity, but these too do not usually involve a complete loss of reason or functioning of the kind that might require psychiatric hospitalization.

However, the fear that we are "losing our minds" is indeed problematic, not because we are likely to "go crazy" (to reiterate, we are not) but because the worry it creates adds a huge amount of stress and distress to our already overburdened coping mechanisms. We are then at risk of developing an array of other psychiatric symptoms that might fall short of a mental breakdown but are nonetheless extremely unpleasant, damaging, and even scary.

Heartbreak Stresses the Brain, the Mind, *and* the Body

As the day of his college girlfriend's departure approached, Dev became more and more concerned about his deteriorating mental health. In his mind, every uncharacteristic incident of rage and sobbing represented him inching another stitch closer to his own proverbial straitjacket.

Dev's friends became concerned as well. They had never seen him behave this way before, and more important, none of them had experienced heartbreak of this magnitude before. Therefore, they had no reference point from which to judge whether his behavior was normative. Consequently, they decided to intervene and address Dev's psychological symptoms using a treatment method favored by many heartbroken young adults—tequila.

"The night my girlfriend left for California, my friends told me they were taking me out to do shots," Dev explained. "I thought it was a great idea. I took the subway up to my friend Andy's house. I was about to change trains when it started—a kind of tightening in my chest. It came on really quickly. Every breath hurt and I couldn't get enough air. I realized I was having a heart attack."

Dev quickly put up his hand to preempt the objection he was sure I was about to make even though I had not moved a muscle. "Yeah, I know, Doc. I was a healthy twenty-two-year-old. No reason I should be having a heart attack. But it totally felt like one. I thought, this is it, I'm going to die!"

Dev managed to get to Andy's apartment. When Andy saw Dev on his doorstep, pale, hyperventilating, and clutching his chest, he took him straight to the emergency room. He was rushed right inside and given a cardiac workup. The doctor then returned with the diagnosis. Dev was not having a heart attack. He was having a panic attack.

Panic attacks cause shallow breathing, tightness in the chest, and an overwhelming sense of doom, which is why so many people who have them end up in the emergency room convinced they're having a heart attack. And while a panic attack is no picnic, having one poses a far less severe threat to our long-term health and longevity than a heart attack does.

That said, Dev's fears were not entirely misplaced. Having our heart broken can actually cause heart failure in rare cases. Known as *broken heart syndrome*, in some individuals, the stress and emotional pain of a breakup can be so severe as to actually cause cardiac abnormalities such as significant chest pain, spasms, and elevated levels of norepinephrine and epinephrine (the fight-or-flight hormones associated with extreme stress) that are at thirty times normal levels. However, despite these commonalities, patients suffering from broken heart syndrome show no evidence of clogged arteries or irreversible heart damage, and they typically recover more quickly than one would from an actual heart attack.

Dev was relieved he had not suffered a heart attack but the incident made him even more convinced he was at risk of going crazy, which only added to his general stress. Heartbreak can make our bodies go into fight-or-flight mode and trigger stress responses that flood our systems with cortisol (the stress hormone). Stress, especially when it is ongoing, impacts our bodies in a variety of damaging ways.

Cortisol makes our immune system function less efficiently. As a result, we are less able to ward off illness and disease and it takes us longer to recover when we do get sick. Indeed, studies have found that heartbreak is associated with suppressed immune system functioning. This is why when we are under periods of intense stress we can feel "run down" and can get a cold or the flu, because our immune systems are not doing their jobs very effectively. Further, chronic stress can impact our cardiovascular functions and digestion and put us at greater risk for heart disease, obesity, and type 2 diabetes.

Stress also taxes our coping mechanisms, thereby lowering our psychological "thresholds," often to the extent that small frustrations, irritations, or disappointments we would usually be able to shrug off pierce our coping mechanisms and elicit greater distress and reactivity. We might open the fridge in the morning, realize we are out of milk and burst into tears, forget our umbrella on a rainy day and feel like screaming in frustration, or get incredibly irritated with a friend or loved one for the smallest infraction. Indeed, over the months it took Dev to get over his breakup, he felt generally run down, lethargic, and was prone to headaches, stomachaches, and upper respiratory illness.

When we catch ourselves thinking and behaving in abnormal ways (for us) in the throes of a broken heart and we worry we might be "losing it," we need to remind ourselves that our wild and vacillating reactions are not signs of mental breakdown but responses to terrible emotional pain. Reassuring ourselves that we are not going crazy and reminding ourselves that our behavior will stabilize once our emotional pain subsides can help us remove at least one layer of stress (the "am I going nuts?" layer) from our already overstressed minds and bodies.

Despite how painful and difficult his breakup was and how worried he had been about losing his mind, Dev truly believed he had gotten over his college girlfriend and moved on. And while in many ways he had, the wounds heartbreak creates are such that even once we've healed, an emotional and psychological vulnerability might still remain. Dev's cyberstalking might have started innocently but by doing it repeatedly over the years, he had inadvertently reopened his old wounds. To close them, he would first have to accept that some of the feelings he had for his old college girlfriend still lingered decades later.

Studies of grieving have found that having catastrophic beliefs about our reactions to heartbreak and what they imply about our character or our mental health are associated with poor or incomplete recoveries. I decided to discuss these research findings with Dev in order to provide him with a framework for understanding why he was still preoccupied with his college girlfriend so many years later. When I suggested he was still dealing with an unresolved grief about his breakup he bristled.

"Unresolved grief? About my college girlfriend? I don't have unresolved grief about her," he insisted. "I don't have any grief about her. I told you, I'm over her."

"And yet you spend hours stalking her online."

"Don't like that word," Dev objected.

"Surveilling her then."

"Sounds worse," Dev responded.

"How does *spying* sound?"

"Fine!" Dev capitulated. "Let's say I stalked her online. I still don't feel grief."

"Okay, you don't feel grief," I agreed. "But how did you feel seeing images and videos of her?" Dev shrugged. I persisted. "Are you telling me you had no emotional reaction at all? No pinch in the heart, no twist in the gut, no pang of longing?"

For the first time, I saw Dev actually take a moment to think back and consider his reaction. "Pinching and twisting no but maybe a pang," he finally admitted.

"There's an emotional wound there that never fully healed," I said. "I'm not saying it's a huge one and I'm not saying it can't heal. But stalking her online is keeping it fresh. And that's not the only way it's hurting you," I added.

Dev cocked his head. "What do you mean?"

"It's not just the stalking that's problematic it's when you choose to do it—when you feel frustrated or upset at the woman you're with at the time. You're using your college girlfriend as an emotional escape hatch instead of channeling your efforts into fixing the problem in your current relationship."

Because so many years had passed since Dev's heartbreak, the tenacity of his negative cognitions was weaker than is often the case when our pain is fresh. As we talked further, he was able to recognize the pattern in his behavior. Stalking his college girlfriend was his way of emotionally disengaging from his current girlfriend when conflict arose—an unconscious way of protecting himself from the potential heartbreak to come.

When we find ourselves revisiting old relationships in our mind (or on our electronic devices), especially ones that ended in heartbreak, we should always consider the context of our current relationship. When we "suddenly" or "coincidently" think of our ex and decide to look him or her up, it is rarely sudden or coincidental. It is usually a reaction to something going on in our present, more specifically in our present relationship. The healthier and more productive response would be to identify what exactly might be irking us at the moment, and to address it with the person with whom we are currently involved rather than to displace those feelings onto figures from our past.

I worked with Dev for several more months during which he deleted his fake accounts and vowed to avoid stalking his college girlfriend in any manner. We were then able to refocus our work on Dev learning more adaptive ways of resolving conflict in his current relationship. His girlfriend moved in several months later.

Heartbreak impacts our minds, our brains, and our bodies in direct, measurable, and unfortunate ways. Sadly, we often respond to these assaults by taking a bad situation and unwittingly making it much worse. As we shall see, to heal from a broken heart we have to first stop making things worse.

# 3 The Many Mistakes That Set Us Back

If there were mental switches we could flip to stop feeling pain and grief when our heart is broken we would obviously flip them. Alas, such switches do not exist. Unfortunately, what do exist are mental switches that make us feel worse, compound our grief, and prolong our recovery. And, although we do so unwittingly, we flip those bad ones all the time.

Perhaps the saddest truth about heartbreak is that in the deepest throes of our grief, the very instincts we rely on to guide us often lead us astray and we are likely to indulge thoughts and behaviors that feel extremely "right" in the moment but are in fact quite psychologically damaging.

## The Importance of Achieving Closure

Kathy, whose boyfriend Rich broke up with her after a romantic weekend in New England, spent countless hours analyzing every nuance of their trip, convinced something must have happened to cause the breakup. Images from their trip constantly popped into her mind unbidden and Kathy pursued each one of these uninvited mental guests, hoping they would lead her to the crucial clue.

But Kathy's entire exploration was founded on two incorrect assumptions. First, she assumed something vital had indeed happened that weekend, something significant enough to cause

Rich to break up with her two weeks later. Yet, Rich had already explained his reasons for the breakup and they not only fit the facts of the relationship they also fit who Rich was as a person.

Despite the anguish the breakup caused her, Kathy still considered Rich a nice guy. Indeed, the one characteristic Kathy and her friends commented on most frequently throughout the relationship was how exceptionally nice and decent Rich was. And he was. Over the six months he dated Kathy, he repeatedly and consistently demonstrated empathy and compassion. His kindness was even evident in how he broke up with her.

Rich explained that he truly liked Kathy and really cared for her. He emphasized that he authentically enjoyed her company (which is why he was able to enjoy a lovely weekend with her so close to the breakup). But after dating Kathy for six months, his feelings for her had simply not progressed sufficiently. As much as he liked Kathy, he wasn't in love with her. Since he wanted to give the relationship every chance to succeed, he suggested the romantic weekend in New England to see if it would tip his feelings for Kathy into the Love column. Once he realized his feelings hadn't changed, he let Kathy know right away. He was well aware of the physical ordeals she already endured and he knew delaying the breakup would only make it more painful for Kathy in the future.

In other words, there was no mystery to be solved. Nothing happened on their romantic weekend that soured Rich on the relationship. Rather, *not enough* happened to change how he felt. Despite both of them having a wonderful time, Rich simply didn't cross an emotional threshold and fall in love.

Kathy's second assumption was even more problematic. She believed whatever went wrong that weekend must have been her fault. Feeling responsible for the demise of the relationship yet not knowing what she had done to cause it only added fuel to her desperate search for answers.

Refusing to accept Rich's perfectly reasonable and logical explanation for the breakup was a huge mistake on Kathy's part, one that significantly impeded her psychological recovery. Studies of romantic breakups have identified a variety of variables that predict healthy emotional adjustment and timely psychological healing. One of the main factors that allows us to let go and move on is having certainty about why the breakup occurred. Having a clear understanding of why things ended helps us reach closure much sooner than we might otherwise. Had Kathy simply accepted Rich's reasons at the time, she could have avoided months of needless mental analysis and intense and prolonged emotional anguish.

### The Dangers of Assuming We Are to Blame

The psychological damage Kathy unwittingly inflicted on herself extended far beyond the mere delay of her recovery. By assuming she was somehow to blame for the demise of the relationship, she was keeping herself stuck in debilitating feelings of loss. When feelings of grief do not ease after six months, it can be a sign that we have developed an abnormal response to loss and heartbreak known as *complicated grief*.

Studies of complicated grief (sometimes called *persistent complex bereavement disorder*) have illuminated the crucial and damaging role of *negative cognitions*. Negative cognitions are inaccurate thoughts or beliefs that make us feel bad about ourselves and prevent us from resuming our lives in a productive way. Psychologically speaking, negative cognitions have three key features: they are self-critical, harmful or limiting; they are inaccurate to some degree (and often significantly so); and most problematic, we tend to be convinced they are true. In fact, in many cases, the thought of questioning the veracity or validity of a negative cognition never even crosses our mind. We just think of them as factual.

Negative cognitions are by no means unusual as it is not uncommon to harbor a few, even if in mild forms. Such erroneous beliefs usually exist side by side with feelings of low self-esteem, depression, anxiety, and of course, heartbreak and grief. Many forms of psychotherapy involve identifying and challenging the patient's negative cognitions as doing so is a proven and highly effective therapeutic technique. There are many forms of negative cognitions. Some tend to be far more damaging than others and put us at risk for developing complicated grief. One of these is excessive self-blame.

Kathy believed she had made a critical mistake, one that led to the end of the relationship. She was entirely unaware that this assumption was completely false and therefore, she had no recognition of the extent to which it sabotaged her ability to move through the grieving process or how it increased her risk of developing both depression and anxiety.

Self-blame is equally common and just as damaging when we lose a cherished pet. We might chastise ourselves for not

realizing sooner that something was wrong, for leaving the cage or window open, for failing to close the gate to the yard, for not anticipating traffic on a quiet street, for not holding their leash tight enough, for not realizing they had eaten something harmful, for not being there for their final moments, or for not appreciating them enough when they were alive.

To be clear, the mere existence of such thoughts does not automatically condemn us to developing complicated grief. The tendency to blame ourselves when our heart is broken is hardly unusual. What matters is how long we allow such feelings to linger. Most of us let go of guilt and regret naturally as we move through the grieving process.

A second negative cognition that has been associated with complicated grief is having extremely negative beliefs about our "self." Lauren, the socially anxious medical student, cried for days after being turned down for a second date. In her eyes, the rejection only reinforced her long-standing insecurities about her appearance. While most of us are likely to focus on our short-comings in the aftermath of a rejection, doing so excessively and catastrophically is problematic. Thoughts such as *I wish I were prettier* or *I don't like my smile* are unfortunate but not unusual, but Lauren verbalized beliefs like *No man will ever want me!* and *I'll be alone forever!*

Since Lauren's maladaptive cognitions occurred in the immediate aftermath of her rejection, she by no means qualified for the diagnosis of complicated grief. But unless she began to question her harsh and punitive self-perceptions, she would certainly be at risk for developing other psychological disorders.

As with all negative self-cognitions, Lauren's by no means reflected an objective reality. She had her profile up on the dating site for less than a week when she scored her first date and by her own admission, she had already been contacted by a dozen men in that time. When I pointed this out to her, she recoiled and asserted she would never date any of them.

However, my point wasn't that Lauren should date those men or that any of them were a good match for her, but that their interest was clear evidence men found her attractive. After all, there were a dozen of them in a single week. Lauren admitted that her friend had also tried to make the same point but, as is often the case with negative self-cognitions, especially ones we have been cultivating for years, Lauren struggled to let go of her self-critical beliefs and dismissed any evidence that contradicted them.

A rule of thumb we should try to live by is that if two different people (other than our parents or grandparents, who are typically the least objective members of our support systems) make the same point (e.g., that people find us attractive or that our ex's rationale for breaking up is reasonable) and it is one we truly bristle at, we should absolutely pause and give it strong consideration. First, because two separate people are saying the same thing, and second because our "bristling" is indicative that our resistance is being fueled by an underlying issue (e.g., we have low self-esteem or we want to keep getting our "fix" by searching for a different rationale) and not by the inherent incorrectness of the assertion.

Why We Idealize the Person Who Broke Our Heart and Why
We Shouldn't

Some years ago I had a first session with a young man who
came to therapy to work on his dating life. He began describing
a party he had recently attended and happened to mention
there were lots of drugs at the party, which he considered a
good thing as he was "fond of cocaine."

Given the casual nature of his admission, I responded in an
equally casual manner, "How fond?"

"Pretty fond," he responded with a wink and a mischievous
smile. "But then a couple of months ago I found out the
cartilage in my left nostril was so damaged from sniffing it, I
had to have surgery to replace it with cartilage from my ear."

"How did that impact your use of cocaine?" I asked
innocently.

"Duh, I use my *right* nostril."

Unaware of the rudeness of his response, he went on to
tell me how great cocaine made him feel and laid out his
arguments for using it, none of which acknowledged the scars
in his nose or ear or the fact that he would soon run out of
healthy nostrils.

People often justify their use of substances by focusing
almost exclusively on how good they feel when they're using,
how much fun they have, and how enjoyable the experience is.
Their cravings for the drug create an idealized perception that
ignores the many terrible mornings and days that follow heavy
usage, how much time and money they spend on the drug, and
the problems it creates in their lives and relationships.

The similarities between addiction and heartbreak are such that our perceptions of the person who broke our heart can become distorted in similar ways. Our "cravings" for them make us focus disproportionately on their best qualities. We replay the greatest hits of wonderful moments we shared (or imagine those we would have shared in the future), we envision their smile, their laugh, and the times they made us feel attractive, happy, and content.

What we focus on much less are their flaws, their annoying habits, the arguments, the tensions, the interests and friendships we gave up to be with them, the times they made us feel terrible about ourselves, the times we cried and were miserable, and the moments we hated their guts and couldn't stand the sight of them.

Natural as it is to do so, by idealizing the person who broke our heart and recalling only highly polished versions of our lives with them, we are actually inflating the magnitude of our loss in our own eyes, exacerbating our emotional pain, and delaying our recovery. Idealizing in this way can easily become a vicious cycle that intensifies our cravings, which in turn reinforces our idealized perceptions, which intensifies our cravings, and so on.

Recently, Gazi, a man in his late thirties, came into his session bereft and announced his girlfriend of nine years had left him. He sat there weeping, barely able to speak. "I thought she would be my wife . . . the mother of my children . . . the woman I grow old with!"

Gazi's emotional pain was very real. What he was saying, not so much. In fact, his girlfriend left him precisely because despite being with her for nine years, he had not felt ready to get married. Further, he had broken up with her at least a dozen times over that period, most recently only a couple of months before she left him. At the time I had suggested to Gazi the pattern of breakups might suggest he had a problem with commitment.

He vehemently disagreed. "How is it a commitment problem? I keep getting back together with her!"

"Exactly," I responded. "You can't commit to the breakups either."

The reality was that commitment issues aside, while he cared for his girlfriend, the relationship just didn't work for him. But in his grief, Gazi pushed aside nine years of hesitation and ambivalence and focused only on the good memories. By doing so he idealized her, as well as the relationship, and that distorted perception then led him to perceive himself as losing someone he was going to marry, when nine years and multiple breakups argued otherwise.

The best way to avoid idealizing the person who broke our heart is to deliberately force a balanced perspective in our mind. We have to remind ourselves of the pet peeves they activated (e.g., their embarrassing eating habits, their chronic lateness, or the bitten fingernail remnants they expectorated onto the coffee table), their different taste in books, sports, or entertainment, your close friends they never got along with, or their defensiveness whenever you tried to have a discussion about a relationship issue. The idea is not to hate them or vilify them but to be able to see their flaws and those of the relationship and not focus exclusively on the good stuff. We often have to remind ourselves of these flaws repeatedly and we should, as doing so will help us let go and ease our worries about never finding someone "as perfect" again.

## How Avoidance Supersizes Grief

When our heart is broken, our efforts to manage the emotional pain we feel can lead us to make decisions that spare us pain in the short term but increase it in the long run. One of the most common ways we seek to limit our emotional distress is to withdraw from people and activities that remind us of what we have lost. However, the longer the relationship lasted, the list of people or situations that remind us of our loss can be rather significant and some of them can be meaningful and important aspects of our lives. Avoiding such people, places, or activities can therefore have a huge impact and throw our entire lives out of whack.

•   •   •

Lindsay, an amateur triathlete and homemaker from New Jersey, used to wake every morning at five thirty, go down to her basement, place her cat, Mittens, on the shelf facing her stationary bike, and work out for forty-five minutes. "Some people like watching TV on the stationary bike," she said to me in our session, "I like watching Mittens. And she watches me back. It's our quality time together."

When Mittens died, Lindsay couldn't stand the thought of doing her morning bike routine without her beloved cat there

to watch her and keep her company. She acknowledged she would not be able to compete at the same level if she only biked outdoors as she was able to do so much less regularly. She also recognized how important competing in triathlons and the fitness her preparation gave her was for her overall physical and mental health. But despite knowing this, she simply could not bring herself to get back on the stationary bike.

What Lindsay did not realize was that by cutting off her indoor bike training and thus limiting her ability to compete, she was at risk of losing far more than just her fitness. Being a triathlete had become an important aspect of Lindsay's self-definition and her fellow competitors represented a significant portion of her social circle. By giving up such meaningful aspects of her life she was not only compounding her grief about Mittens, she was seriously jeopardizing her mental health.

Although it might seem necessary or prudent to avoid that which evokes painful associations of our loss, doing so is rarely wise. A general rule of human psychology is that avoiding things does not lessen their emotional impact on us—it super-sizes it. By avoiding her basement Lindsay wasn't lessening the association between her stationary bike and Mittens, she was making it stronger. I worried that if she continued to avoid her bike the association with Mittens might spread and contaminate other aspects of her triathlon training.

Indeed, this kind of post-heartbreak avoidance often starts small and then spreads, forcing us to continually narrow our spheres of operation as a result, sometimes in impractical and even ludicrous ways. For example, Kathy refused to go to any restaurant she had been to with Rich, as doing so would be too painful a reminder of the breakup. But given how frequently they dined out during their six-month relationship, Kathy's list of "prohibited" establishments covered a huge swath of Manhattan real estate. She should have been finding ways to diminish Rich's presence in her daily thoughts. Instead her avoidance was making it virtually impossible to escape his shadow.

When places and people become too tightly associated with our broken heart, we need to "cleanse" our associations and reclaim them. The best way to do so is by revisiting these places under different and specific circumstances so we can create new associations for them. For example, I suggested to Kathy that she reclaim the brunch place she used to go to with Rich by turning it into the brunch place she now goes to with her friends. I warned her that her first or second outings there would still be haunted by memories of Rich but by the third or fourth visit, the new associations would start to become strong enough to compete with the old ones.

When trying to replace old and painful associations with new ones, we have to be careful about one thing. We must avoid reinforcing the old associations. Consequently, I advised Kathy to avoid mentioning Rich when at the brunch place, and as much as possible, to avoid even thinking about him.

### Holding on to Reminders Can Keep Us Holding on to Pain

Rigidly avoiding reminders of our loss can lead us to forgo important aspects of our lives but holding on to them too tightly can be just as problematic. Roughly four months after Ben's dog, Bover, died, he called me prior to our session to let me know he had been delayed by a last-minute conference call with his boss and he would not be able to get to my office in time. He asked if we could do the session via a video call. I agreed.

Ben's computer was situated in the corner of his living room. Consequently, I had a clear view of his living room and the adjacent open kitchen. Ben began catching me up on his latest clash with his boss but I barely heard a word. I was totally distracted by what I saw behind him. There, at the foot of Ben's small dining table, were Bover's food and water bowls.

I waited for an opening and asked Ben about it. He sheepishly tilted his laptop down to show me that Bover's large flat cushion was still at the foot of his workstation. He also admitted that Bover's brush and comb remained in the kitchen drawer with his other grooming tools, and that his leash still hung on the coatrack by the front door.

Ben was no stranger to grief. He had experienced significant loss twice before when his parents died. I had worked with him at that time and knew he was well aware that holding on to too many vivid reminders could make those losses feel perpetually fresh and painful. By living with Bover's things all around him, Ben was preventing the "psychological scabs" time creates from forming over his emotional wound.

That said, I did understand why he was doing it.

When we lose someone we often hold on to their clothes and the objects we associate with them because removing them feels disloyal. Similarly, when a beloved pet dies, putting away their toys and grooming instruments, disposing of remaining food, and removing their crates, cages, or pillows can feel like an impossible task. The mere thought of doing so can evoke powerful feelings of guilt. We feel like we are betraying an animal that had been unconditionally loyal to us throughout their lives. It can even feel as though we're disrespecting their memory.

Ben felt all those things. He rationalized holding on to those reminders by telling himself he would put Bover's things away when he felt ready to do so. A part of him knew that having Bover's things around him was actually preventing him from feeling "ready," but with each passing day, the thought of disposing of Bover's possessions felt more and more impossible.

A similar drama often plays out when our heart is broken by romantic love. Some of us cling to every reminder we have, surrounding ourselves with the evidence of what we once had but lost. And some of us prefer to dispose of all reminders as quickly as possible, to erase every trace of the person who broke our heart and of our time with them.

Although these are entirely opposite approaches, one is not necessarily better or healthier than the other, at least not initially. Whether we choose to eliminate reminders or hoard them in the immediate aftermath of a breakup or loss reflects our first reactions, our emotional reflex. The question is what we do past that moment.

Reminders are psychological representations of our emotional attachment to the pet we lost or the person who broke our heart. As we process our loss and move through our

grief, this attachment should weaken with time. Disposing of reminders reflects our willingness to let go and our readiness to move on. If months later we are still keeping too many of them, it can be a sign we have become stuck.

Getting rid of these reminders will certainly feel torturous in the moment but this is one of those times we need to pay a short-term price for a long-term gain. The vast majority of people I've worked with report feeling a significant reduction in emotional pain and a big improvement in mood in the days following a "reminder purge." How many reminders we choose to keep, if any, depends on whether we can do so while still letting go and moving forward.

Those who prefer to eliminate all reminders early on face a different complication. While it is easy enough to locate physical reminders in our home, car, or office, virtual reminders typically exist in multiple locations. Between our social media accounts, digital photos, blogs, texts, e-mails, dating sites, and other warehouses of digital information, finding and purging them can be a tricky task indeed.

•   •   •

I recently worked with Svetlana, a nurse in her thirties. Svetlana met a man on a popular dating app and they went out for several months. Things began to go badly and the relationship deteriorated rapidly, leading to her boyfriend making an abrupt exit. Heartbroken, Svetlana quickly fell into the familiar trap of idealizing her ex and convincing herself he was "the one." We spent weeks working on her recognizing his faults and the flaws in their relationship (both of which were numerous), and slowly she regained a more balanced perspective.

A couple of months after the breakup Svetlana felt ready to date again. Since she did not want to run across her ex's profile, she canceled her membership to the site she had met him on and joined two newer dating sites instead. The first immediately sent her a list of five potential matches. She swiped left when she saw the first two (i.e., she was not interested). The third profile was that of her ex. She canceled her membership. A week later, the second app sent her their weekly list of "great matches!" and there again was her ex's smiling face.

"I knew he was the perfect man for me," Svetlana sobbed, when she told me about it, "and every matchmaking algorithm out there agrees! I know he wasn't perfect but . . . the universe is telling me he was the one!"

"May I please see one of your profiles?" I asked.

"Why?" Svetlana asked.

"Because I'm wondering how you described the person you were looking for." Svetlana brought up her profile and handed me her phone. Sure enough, every descriptor she had listed matched her ex perfectly, including height, weight, hair and eye color, profession, and hobbies.

I handed her back the phone and said, "The universe is only telling you what you told it. It's not the algorithms, it's you."

Svetlana nodded. She had not even realized she was doing it. Indeed, I have worked with numerous people who joined dating sites after getting divorced only to see their ex-wives and ex-husbands show up as suggested matches. Such incidents reflect the consistency of our tastes much more than they do divine intervention.

These days, digital reminders of our broken hearts can easily haunt our filing and storage systems. We innocently click on a file and discover a photo album we had forgotten existed. These kinds of unexpected virtual encounters can be both painful and shocking. Some of us might react by quickly clicking delete but others might be tempted into a painful trip down memory lane that only reactivates hurt feelings and heartache we might have already put behind us.

Social media platforms are even more problematic in this regard. The person who broke our heart often remains connected to people we know, making it possible for their updates and posts to be shared by third parties and show up in our feeds.

Another major complication of heartbreak in the digital age is the reaction to the breakup among our friends and followers on social media. A recent study examined how breakups play out on Twitter. One of the phenomena the researchers observed was batch "unfollowing." People often lost fifteen to twenty followers in the immediate aftermath of a breakup as friends took sides and dropped one member of the couple in favor of the other. A similar phenomenon occurs on Facebook where a breakup can be followed by a large drop in the number of a person's "friends."

Social media users are often extremely cognizant of their follower numbers as these statistics represent not just the size of our social circles but our sphere of influence and our relative importance in the social media world. Such batch losses can easily add hurt and embarrassment to an already painful breakup. If losing followers and friends is important to us, we should take the time to replenish by reaching out to new people and inviting them to follow, friend, or connect with us. Seeing our numbers go back to where they were can, at least slightly, ease our distress.

As for losing friends to the breakup, the reality of breakups is such that friends will indeed choose sides, either because our ex expresses an expectation to that effect, or because they think the other person would want them to do so. Therefore, in some cases, it might be possible to reach out to some of the people who unfriended us and let them know we would like to stay connected. Although we risk getting turned down by doing so, we might be pleasantly surprised by their response, especially if the breakup was not acrimonious.

Avoiding the typical mistakes we make when our heart is broken will help prevent us from slipping backwards or getting stuck on our journey to recovery. Breaking these kinds of damaging habits is hugely important as is the need to adopt healing ones. However, in order to take the final steps toward fixing our broken heart, we must be willing to make one crucial decision—to let go.

# 4 Healing Starts in the Mind

Broken hearts are engines of endless psychological paradox. We want nothing more than to end our emotional pain, yet we indulge thoughts and behaviors that only deepen it. We feel dismissed, rejected, and abandoned, yet idealize the person who caused those feelings. We're desperate to move past our grief, yet we tenaciously hold on to reminders and keepsakes that keep us submerged in it.

Why does heartbreak ensnare us in so many paradoxes?

To answer this question we must first revisit our evolutionary past. Generally speaking, our body's priority is always to heal and keep us alive. When we get physically injured, we do not have to make a conscious decision to heal as our body does so spontaneously. But our mind's priority is not to repair bone and tissue but to keep us away from situations that have hurt us in the past. The more painful an experience is, the harder our mind will work to make sure we do not make that "mistake" again.

To that end, when our heart is broken, our mind tries to keep our pain fresh and unforgettable by having thoughts and images of our loss pop into our heads when we least expect them. It makes sure to flood us with anxiety and stress when we consider dating again, and to infuse us with guilt if we are tempted to get another pet after losing one we had cherished. But while our mind wants us to make sure we do not forget, to recover from heartbreak we need to be able to do just that. We need to decrease the time we spend dwelling on our loss and reduce the importance it has in our thoughts and our lives.

This simple "conflict of interest" between our unconscious mind and our conscious goals is hugely important. If we wish to heal more quickly and completely, we need to take deliberate action to override the damaging dictates of our unconscious mind and adopt new habits to bolster our emotional health. Doing so is very different from the current belief so many of us have about heartbreak that asserts we need only let time do its work. Time will do its work, but it will do it slowly and often ineffectively, and it can leave us with wounds that never fully healed.

Our bodies heal well automatically. Our minds do not.

However, this mental "disadvantage" also has a bright side. While we cannot command white blood cells to attack a virus or instruct our bones to heal, we can affect what happens in our mind if we are sufficiently determined to do so. There is a vast difference between *wanting* our emotional pain to stop and making a firm decision to *make* it stop. Wishing we could move on is not the same as resolving to do so. To fully heal when our heart is broken, we have to look in the mirror (metaphorically and perhaps literally) and tell ourselves it's time to let go.

And that can be extremely difficult.

### The Many Different Ways We Need to Let Go

What makes letting go so challenging is that we need to let go of far more than mere emotional pain—we need to let go of hope, of the fantasy in which we undo what went wrong, of the psychological presence the person or pet has in our daily thoughts, and thus, in our lives. We need to truly say good-bye—to turn away from love, even when there is no longer a person or animal there to receive it. And we need to let go of a part of ourselves, of the person we were when our love still mattered.

Kathy was addicted to her memories of Rich. Her mind justified her indulging them by creating a false narrative—that something had happened during their romantic weekend together that caused the breakup. To move on, Kathy had to make the same decision every addict must if they wish to turn their lives around and escape the clutches of the substance that controls them. She would have to give up her quest for answers—her "drug"—and go cold turkey.

In order to do so, Kathy needed to be ready to manage the powerful cravings and intense withdrawal that would try to break her resolve. She would have to conquer the powerful urges that would compel her to revisit her memories and get one more taste of the happiness she had felt that weekend. She would have to anticipate the many excuses and justifications her mind would concoct to entice her back into her old habits and be ready to argue against them.

Letting go was an equally torturous decision for Ben. Ben's dog, Bover, had been exquisitely attuned to his moods—his ability to recognize when Ben needed comfort and affection was remarkable. To Ben, holding on to Bover's possessions was a way of returning the loyalty Bover had shown him for so many years.

To move on, Ben would have to give up the reminders that cluttered his apartment and kept Bover's memory fresh. He would have to tolerate intense feelings of disloyalty and harness every ounce of emotional determination he had to withstand the emotional tidal wave of guilt that was sure to come. He would have to realize those were distortions his mind created to keep him from moving on, that his debt to Bover had already been paid.

Ben bristled when I suggested as much. "Bover was far more loyal to me than I was to him. He was devoted to me!"

"He was devoted," I agreed. "But your devotion to him was ever greater. You were his owner. Bover had no one else to focus his loyalty on. You did, at least theoretically. Yet you chose to be devoted only to him."

Ben looked at me confused. "Huh? Who else *could* I have been loyal to?"

"A woman."

"Oh," Ben responded.

"Ben, you barely dated since your divorce. Wasn't Bover the reason? Wasn't there a part of you that felt he was enough? Wasn't there a part of you that refrained from getting emotionally attached to another person out of loyalty to Bover?"

Ben sat back and thought for a moment. "Dating sucks."

"It can," I said.

"And Bover was so loving and affectionate and consistent." Ben sighed. "He *was* enough."

"Yes, he was. His memory is not. Ben, you repaid your debt of loyalty to Bover while he was alive, many times over. Now you have to be loyal to yourself, to your own needs and happiness."

Ben recognized what he had to do but that didn't make it any less painful. The next day, he took all of Bover's possessions and placed them in a box, weeping as he did it. He was finally on the path of healing but I knew we had more work to do.

### The Power of Self-Compassion

Lauren, who felt crushed after her first date in years rejected her, was caught in a paradox that ensnares many who suffer romantic disappointment. She believed her only chance for happiness depended on finding a partner yet she was too terrified and pessimistic to try dating again. In an effort to protect herself from further heartache, Lauren's mind convinced her she was too unattractive to ever find love, so there was no point to trying.

To heal and move on, Lauren had to be willing to let go of her self-critical convictions and adopt a new mental habit, one that would limit her self-loathing and build her confidence: *self-compassion*.

Self-compassion involves developing a nonjudgmental inner voice that responds to our own suffering with kindness and caring rather than self-blame. Practicing it involves replacing self-critical thoughts with supportive and compassionate ones. It requires us to respond to our mistakes with patience and under-standing, recognizing that erring is a part of being human. We can certainly acknowledge our mistakes and shortcomings but we should not chastise and punish ourselves for them. Doing so

yields no insights and it has a terrible impact on our self-esteem, confidence, and overall emotional health.

When I suggested Lauren adopt the practice of self-compassion she was naturally hesitant. *Behavioral* habit change is hard enough. Changing our *mental* habits is harder. Switching her thinking to a diametrically opposed track would require Lauren to make a firm decision and then back it up with a serious dollop of motivation and willpower. I had faith in Lauren's willpower. The sticking point for her was the initial decision to change.

Since she was a medical student, I decided to share with her some recent research findings. I told her about studies that investigated the impact of self-compassion on our mental health. The findings were significant and had been replicated many times. Practicing self-compassion increases self-esteem, improves psychological and social functioning, lowers depression and anxiety, enhances emotional health, and bestows an array of other psychological benefits.

Lauren was intrigued. She accepted that self-compassion worked for some people, she just didn't know if it was something she would be able to do. Seeing as she had opened the door, I suggested some specific techniques. Scientists have found that one way to increase our self-compassion is to be compassionate toward others. For example, in one study, the mere act of writing a comforting message to a heartbroken stranger increased the self-compassion with which participants regarded a negative incident from their own past.

Another technique to limit self-critical thoughts is to imagine ourselves saying those thoughts aloud to a dear friend who was hurting. Most of us would recoil at the notion of being so cruel to a friend in need—a stark reminder that we should recoil just as much when we direct the same critical words toward ourselves.

"Okay, I'll try it," Lauren finally agreed.

Since she was a self-confessed nerd, I decided to quote Yoda. "There is no try."

Well versed in *Star Wars*, Lauren nodded and said, "Do or do not."

I cautioned Lauren that practicing self-compassion requires both patience and mindfulness. It is easy to slip into our old ways of thinking and resurrect our self-critical inner voice and we need to be on guard and catch ourselves when we do so. All habit change is effortful at first, but usually after about a month of daily practice, the habit becomes more ingrained.

For Lauren, it took five weeks of daily mindfulness and attention. She posted stickers all around her apartment reminding her to be compassionate toward herself. She put self-compassionate motifs on her home screen on her phone and laptop. And she even made up a silly ditty to hum to herself (the only line she disclosed was "I ain't wearin' no self-swearin', self-compassion, my new fashion").

Her abilities as a songwriter aside, Lauren's approach is a good example of the lengths to which we need to go if we truly want to change our way of thinking. Without the many visual reminders (fine, and the song), it would have been hard for her to remain consistent and get the new habit ingrained enough to become self-sustaining.

Happily, Lauren's efforts paid off. The change I saw in her over time was remarkable, especially in her self-esteem. When our heart is broken and our self-esteem has taken a severe blow, what we need most is to revive it. We should heal ourselves by focusing on our best qualities, everything we have to offer that a potential relationship partner would appreciate. And yet too often we do the opposite—focus on every shortcoming we have and on all the reasons we believe we are likely to be rejected again in the future.

Lauren had been an expert at shooting her self-esteem in the foot (if not the heart). I therefore insisted she start every session by listing five good qualities she had to offer in the dating world without repeating ones she had already used. While she could barely get any out at first, with each passing week she got more comfortable. Once she was able to deliver her list confidently and without any qualifiers, I knew she was ready to start dating again.

Lauren did too. She reactivated her profile on the dating site soon thereafter.

## Recognizing New Voids and Filling Them

Ben had finally removed Bover's pillow, bowls, and leash from view, but his emotional recovery was by no means complete. He used to take Bover to a dog run every morning before he began work. Bover had regular playmates there and Ben had become friendly with their owners. He sat and chatted with them for thirty minutes to an hour while their dogs played, much as parents and nannies do when taking their children to a playground. Ben had a limited circle of friends and his "dog-run clutch" had formed a meaningful chunk of his social life. Now that Bover was gone, he often went days without having a face-to-face conversation with another person.

We usually perceive the loss of a beloved pet as creating a void in our lives. What we often do not realize is that it creates far more than one.

Once Ben recognized how many voids Bover's death had left, he agreed he had to find ways to fill them. But he couldn't think of a single hobby, activity, or pastime that held any appeal. There was simply nothing in which he wanted to invest time and effort. He felt entirely stumped.

"Okay, so there are no passions or interests that grab you," I said to him in our next session. "I can think of only one option then. You need another warm body back in your life."

"I'm not ready to get another dog!" Ben interrupted.

"Again, I meant a woman."

Again Ben said, "Oh."

Ben finally relented and agreed to post a profile on a dating app. He specified one important condition in his profile. The woman he was looking for had to love dogs. Over the next couple of months, Ben went on a few dates, none of which yielded a second. But spending time messaging various women and occasionally meeting them for dates went a long way toward filling some of the voids in his life. His mood improved, as did his work. And for the first time since Bover died, his boss actually complimented him on an assignment.

We stopped working together shortly after. I don't know whether Ben found a new relationship or whether he ever got another dog. I would like to think he did both. I do believe that if his heart gets broken again in the future, he will reach out to me. And much as I am curious to know how he's doing, for that reason alone, I hope I never hear from him again.

### Using Mindfulness to Battle Rumination
Studies of how heartbroken people heal have revealed the importance of attaining closure in achieving timely and healthy adjustment. Specifically, in order to move on, we have to reach a solid understanding of why the breakup occurred. As we've seen, being clear about the *why* helps us let go of our hopes and fantasies of reconciliation and attain closure. But what do we do when our questions cannot be answered?

Breakups are often cruel. We come home to empty apartments, receive a terse text message, or find out our ex has changed their relationship status to single on a social media platform. Even when we are given the courtesy of an explanation, it is often insufficient (e.g., *I have finals coming up so it's not a good time for me to be in a relationship*), vague (e.g., *It's not you it's me*), uninformative (e.g., *I'm just not in the right place*), or unjustly accusatory (e.g., *I just can't deal with how emotional you get when I yell at you!*).

Many of us try to extract a clearer or more honest response from the person who broke our heart but such efforts rarely succeed. Perhaps it is best they do not. Whatever explanation the other person offers will not change the bottom line: they felt we were incompatible in some way. Further, pursuing a more complete answer is likely to make us emotionally vulnerable and open the door to feeling hurt, enraged, frustrated, or bewildered all over again.

Instead, we should come up with our own explanation for why the breakup occurred—a best guess that fits the facts, considers the personality and past behavior of our ex, takes the context of the breakup and recent history into account, and most important, leaves our pride, dignity, and self-esteem intact. If we have to fill in the blanks ourselves, we might as well do so in a way that makes us feel better about things, not worse, a rationale we can sell both to ourselves and to others.

A good example of a worthy breakup rationale is the one Rich gave Kathy (he cared for Kathy and enjoyed her company tremendously but he had just not fallen in love). His reasons were measured, nonjudgmental, and compassionate—a rare thing in the world of heartbreak—which is why it was so unfortunate Kathy chose to reject his explanation and launch a six-month quest for an alternative one.

By that point Kathy could no longer deny how stuck she was. She was finally willing to consider the futility of her search and accept what Rich had told her. Doing so was by no means an easy decision. She was still consumed by an obsessive urge to ruminate about Rich, compelled by the reward circuitry in her brain that created withdrawal symptoms that were hard to withstand.

Once we spend weeks and months stewing about our ex, quitting the habit cold turkey can be extremely challenging. Fortunately, there are psychological techniques that are effective in countering this kind of obsessive rumination.

Rumination involves a repetitious focus on negative thoughts and memories of all kinds (not just related to heartbreak) that can easily become habitual and lead to elevated risk of clinical depression. They key to breaking free of rumination is to counteract its negative pull by fostering ways of thinking that are strictly nonjudgmental. The most potent and successful of these techniques is called *mindfulness meditation.*

Mindfulness meditation involves focusing on our internal states and experiences in the present. One can do so in a variety of ways. We can focus on the sensation of air entering our lungs, the smells around us as we breathe, how the wind or the sun feel against our face, the patterns cracks make in the sidewalks and streets we walk on, or the different hues of green in the plants and trees we pass on our walk. Whenever our attention is drawn to an unrelated thought (e.g., *I can't believe my ex dumped me!*) we simply note the thought nonjudgmentally (e.g., *I had a thought about my ex*) and bring our awareness back to our present experience.

Mindfulness meditation is a form of cognitive training (like a workout for your mind), much like self-compassion is. As such, it requires daily practice. Beginners might experience intrusive thoughts regularly and spend most of their time bringing their focus back to their breathing. But the more we practice, the longer we will be able to stay within our meditative focus and the disruptions of negative (and other) thoughts will decline.

Mindfulness is not just a form of meditation. It is a way of thinking and being in which we choose to focus on our experience of the present—the scents of the different flowers as we stroll through a park, the song of the birds outside our window as we rest in a chair, or the noises of a busy street as we walk to work.

Mindfulness has been extensively studied in recent years. Directing attention to our present experience rather than ruminating about the past or worrying about the future has been demonstrated to have significant psychological benefits such as reducing stress, distractibility, rumination, and obsessional thinking.

I instructed Kathy on the basics of mindfulness training and suggested she practice at least five times a week. Given how severe her ruminating had become I expected her progress to be slow. But only five weeks later she came into the session and announced, "Good news."

Kathy's ultimate goal was to go an entire week without thinking about Rich. It was a big ask. Was it possible she had already achieved it?

"I didn't think of Rich for six hours!" she said.

I was certainly encouraged by the fact that Kathy went six hours without thinking about Rich but what encouraged me even more was her enthusiasm. Apparently, her initial skepticism about the technique had diminished and she was ready to get serious.

And she did.

Kathy's powerful determination—that which had been channeled into getting her through cancer treatments only to be diverted into fueling her ruminative quest to solve the (nonexistent) riddle of her breakup—came back. Once again Kathy harnessed her motivation and perseverance to improve her health—this time her mental health.

She signed up for mindfulness meditation classes, she read books about it, joined a meetup group, recruited two of her friends to practice with her, and downloaded endless lectures and podcasts on the subject.

Mindfulness meditation does not just reduce rumination and self-criticism. It can also lower our emotional reactivity to distressing thoughts or events such that even when the same old harmful thoughts do come up, they pack less punch. Indeed, Kathy not only had fewer intrusive thoughts about Rich, she also found the ones she did have to be less upsetting and easier to banish.

I next saw Kathy after several weeks and the change in her was noticeable. Finally, she no longer looked like she was in continual pain.

"I'm loving the mindfulness meditation," Kathy said, "but it's possible I went a little overboard. My friends thought I was just substituting one addiction with another."

"Did you agree?" I asked.

"A bit," she admitted. "So I decided to continue the daily meditations but drop the evening classes. I was thinking of dropping them anyway. I needed to free up some time."

"For . . . ?" I asked.

Kathy took out her phone and showed me a text she had sent to her friends the night before: *I'm ready!*

"It's Raining Men" began playing in my head. I sat back and said, "Hallelujah!"

## Recovering Who We Are

All relationships require us to modify how we see ourselves. We change our pronoun use and substitute *I* and *my* with *we* and *our*, we gravitate toward socializing with other couples and see single friends less often, we give up individual interests and adopt mutual ones, we modify the products we use, we change our habits both in the home and outside it, and the list goes on. When our relationship ends we then have to readjust and reconnect to who we are as individuals.

Numerous studies have found that recovering our sense of self and getting in touch with our core is a crucial variable in our ability to heal from heartbreak. One recent study examined changes in participants' self-concept and emotional well-being over an eight-week period following a breakup. Researchers measured participants' self-concept and psychological well-being using both questionnaires and facial electromyography (fEMG). A fEMG measures tiny changes in facial muscles that are indicative of an emotional response but are not discernable to the naked eye.

Together, the two methods confirmed that when people whose hearts were broken failed to redefine their sense of self, their adjustment to the breakup was poorer and they experienced greater psychological distress. The same was true of participants who exhibited strong emotional reactions to thoughts of their partner. The researchers concluded that one of the reasons we struggle to redefine our sense of self after a breakup is because we are (unconsciously) continuing to define ourselves by our (now defunct) relationship.

Reconnecting to who we are is an equally vital task when we lose a cherished pet. When Lindsay's cat, Mittens, died, she lost a vital aspect of her identity. Lindsay had always defined herself as a mother, a wife, and an athlete. Her role as a mother was clearly the most important to her and although she would never admit it, her role as an athlete had always been a close second.

Lindsay continued to work out but while she maintained her running and swimming schedules, she barely biked at all. However, biking had been her strongest leg in the triathlon, the one to which she felt most connected. Her next big race was supposed to take place less than a month after Mittens died. A few days before the race, Lindsay told me she had decided to drop out.

"I used to be an athlete," she said, "but since Mittens died—"

"Wait, wait, wait," I interrupted. "You *used* to be an athlete? Is it acceptable to you that you no longer are?"

"No, but it's a reality."

"The only reality is that Mittens died," I responded. "That reality you can't change. But whether you are an athlete, whether you give up the sport you love is not a reality, it's a choice."

Lindsay was making a mistake many of us make when faced with the task of redefining ourselves in the face of grief. She was looking to her actions to define who she was rather than deciding who she wanted to be and figuring out which actions supported that self-definition. I urged Lindsay to figure out how she might continue her training, as triathlons played a key role in her life, one she could not afford to lose.

She agreed to consider the idea. So I decided to push her a little further. I told her there was a relevant research finding, a single variable that has repeatedly predicted healthier and quicker emotional adjustments to heartbreak. But it is one that most people balk at: finding a replacement for the pet (or person) they have lost.

To be clear, going out on dates when our heart has been broken and getting a new pet after we lose a beloved one can feel inappropriate, premature, awkward, disloyal, unwise, unfair, and just plain wrong. And yet, doing so has been shown to effectively ease both emotional pain and grief because it reduces our attachment to the person or pet we lost.

Of course, time is a factor as well. Should Kathy have rushed out and started dating the day after Rich broke up with her? No. Should Ben have left the vet's after Bover died and gone right to the local animal shelter to get another dog? No. But we do not have to wait until we are "totally over it" to take such steps either.

We might not be entirely emotionally available when we first start dating after a difficult breakup, but if we met someone we were interested in getting to know further we can always let him or her know we need to take things slowly.

Similarly, getting another pet does not mean we should abandon our thoughts and memories of the one that died. Our hearts are big enough to mourn one animal while still being able to care for another. It might take us longer to fall in love with our new pet when we're still grieving the old one but only a little. Pets are usually quite adept at finding their way into an animal lover's heart.

Lindsay was spared the decision of whether she was ready to get another cat. Apparently, I was not the only one who felt she needed to get back to her training and embrace her role as a triathlete. A few weeks later, her husband and kids surprised her on her birthday with a big box with holes on top. Inside was a new kitten. The next morning, Lindsay took the kitten down to the basement, placed it on the shelf, and got on her bike.

•   •   •

Recovering from heartbreak always starts with a decision, a determination to move on when our mind is fighting to keep us stuck. The battle ahead requires courage and determination but also knowledge and awareness:

- We have to understand the ways our mind is working against us and take steps to counter the unhealthy urges and habits that are setting us back.

- We have to fight the addictive tendency to keep those whom we have lost in our lives, whether via memories or reminders.

- We have to rebuild our self-esteem by practicing self-compassion.

- We have to adopt mindfulness to battle obsessive thoughts of our loss.

- We have to recognize the voids that have been created in our lives and take steps to fill them.

- We have to reconnect to our core so we can get back in touch with the essence of what makes us who we are.

Our heart might be broken but we do not have to break with it. We can fight back and move on when sufficient time has passed even if we do not feel ready to do so. We can take control of our lives and our minds and put ourselves on the path to healing. Emotional pain should not and need not be a constant companion.

Do not let it become one.

# Making Emotional Pain Visible

I have worked with scores of heartbroken people over the past twenty years and I remember many of them vividly. This is not surprising, as the ease with which we recall events is heavily influenced by their intensity, and the raw emotion and terrible anguish of a person whose heart just got broken is hard to forget. This is especially true when the patient sitting across from me is a teenager. The hormone-fueled intensity of adolescence, the already heightened emotions that go with it, and their inexperience and innocence, render teenagers exquisitely vulnerable to the agony of heartbreak.

One teenage patient in particular stands out in my mind because his story encapsulated almost everything that is wrong with how we currently regard heartbreak. Greg was a highly intelligent, gay seventeen-year-old junior who had recently come out at school—thankfully, to relatively little fanfare. Whereas straight high school kids have a wide range of romantic options from which to choose, LGBTQ youth typically face a much sparser selection. Greg spent two years nursing a crush on Devon, a senior and one of only two other out gay kids in his school.

A month after coming out, Greg finally gathered the courage to walk up to Devon during lunch and suggest they hang out. As happens far too often with teenagers, Devon's rejection was both swift and unnecessarily cruel. Feeling both humiliated and absolutely gutted, Greg made his way to his history class, in which he was scheduled to have a big exam. Greg's best friend (who was straight) always sat next to Greg in history and Greg hoped to have a few moments to talk with his buddy and get support before the exam began.

But when Greg arrived in class, his friend was not there. As he later found out, his friend had twisted his ankle while shooting hoops during the lunch break. When the history teacher saw the swollen ankle, she excused him from the test and sent him to the nurse's office for treatment. Alone and with no support, Greg spent the hour fighting tears while struggling to focus on his exam. Knowing he had done poorly (indeed he had failed), Greg approached the history teacher after class to explain why he had trouble concentrating during the test. But instead of responding with empathy or compassion, Greg's teacher chastised him for "making excuses."

This is the message we're sending high school kids about emotional versus physical pain. If your ankle swells even slightly, your physical discomfort will be noticed and you will be afforded both compassion and consideration. But if your heart gets ripped out of your chest and the emotional pain you feel is so severe you can't even concentrate, you will be given neither. If this is how we educate our youth, is it any surprise that heartbreak is so poorly understood, that emotional pain is so often ignored? And if nothing in her schooling or training gave her any tools to deal with students whose heart just got broken, should we be surprised by Greg's teacher responding as she did?

I am not advocating we excuse every teenager who claims to have a broken heart from taking exams. Given how frequently teenagers get their hearts broken we would end up with more students sitting out exams than taking them. Yes, separating the normative psychological and emotional distress adolescents experience on a daily basis from an exceptional, urgent, or acute situation is by no means an easy call. But Greg was not someone nursing his hurt feelings from a rejection or breakup that happened days or weeks previously. He was an A student, blinking back tears in obvious emotional pain.

We desperately need a more open dialogue about how severely heartbreak impacts our emotions and functioning. And for such discussions to be productive, we have to disavow ourselves of the notion that there is something childish, embarrassing, or inappropriate about feeling severe emotional anguish when our heart is broken because heartbreak is devastating, at any age.

We suffer emotional pain that is nearly "unbearable" for days, weeks, and even months on end. Our body experiences stresses that can damage both our short-term and long-term health. Our grief activates circuitry in our brain that causes withdrawal symptoms similar to those experienced by people who are addicted to cocaine or heroin. Our ability to focus and concentrate, think creatively, problem-solve, and generally function at our regular capacity becomes significantly impaired. Our lives are thrown upside down, leaving us questioning who we are and how to define ourselves going forward.

The fact that all this goes virtually unrecognized if not entirely ignored by society at large makes our ordeal far more challenging than it already is. Our individual friends and loved ones might offer us comfort and support but only for a limited time. Our schools, institutions, workplaces, and even our healthcare system fail to do even that (the kind actions of some individual bosses or employers notwithstanding).

What makes this state of affairs so unfortunate and truly unacceptable is that we are not fundamentally blind to grief. When a first-degree relative dies, especially if it is a spouse, parent, or child (siblings are last on the list), we are usually afforded time off, sympathy, compassion, and even a tacit understanding that we will not be functioning at our best as we grieve. Similarly, employers are likely to be at least supportive and sympathetic when we let them know we're going through a rough divorce. Our grief, in such cases, is both recognized and sanctioned, regardless of its magnitude.

But other kinds of grief, such as the kinds of heartbreak we've explored here, is neither recognized nor sanctioned, it is disenfranchised, regardless of how emotionally devastated we are. Not only are we robbed of support and compassion, we are forced to expend our dwindling emotional reserves to hide how bereft we feel lest we be judged for being overly emotional, immature, or weak of character.

My concern about how we marginalize these kinds of grief is not just a reflection of my work with heartbroken patients. Studies of disenfranchised grief, and there are many of them, have found that when societies do not sanction grief, we internalize these standards and regard our own emotions and reactions as less legitimate. This lack of external and internal validation has also been found to negatively impact our psychosocial health and increase our risk for developing clinical depression.

If emotional pain were visible, heartbreak and the suffering it caused would not remain disenfranchised for long. When we show up to work or school with a broken leg, arm, or even a broken finger, we often garner more attention, concern, and consideration, because we can see the splints or bandages, than we are likely to when our heart is broken. They are there as evidence that we hurt. And yet, broken bones inflict none of the profound cognitive, emotional, and psychological impairments heartbreak does.

Most companies are hesitant to institutionalize sanctioned allowances for "emotional health reasons" (short of major mental diagnoses) because they fear employees will unfairly take advantage of them. However, their assumptions are both shortsighted and misguided. By not affording employees the time and support they need to heal, companies are left carrying the burden of less productive employees who are functioning below their capacity for extended durations of time.

If companies recognized the debilitating impact of heartbreak and gave their employees time to grieve, get support, and recover, it would allow employees to return to full productivity sooner than they might otherwise. Rather than hide our emotional pain from our fellow students and colleagues, teachers and employers, we could heal it more quickly and minimize our periods of compromised productivity.

If schools accepted the basic fact that emotional pain is just as important, legitimate, and debilitating as physical pain, they could train their educators to be more supportive of and compassionate toward students suffering from heartbreak. There is no reason why we do not teach our captive audience of middle and high school students how to avoid the mistakes that make our emotional pain worse and how to adopt the habits that promote emotional health and healing. But we do not.

If emotional pain were visible we would all conduct ourselves very differently. We would find kinder ways to break up with the person we were dating and we would be less cruel when rejecting people who expressed interest in us. We would show more concern when we saw someone sitting alone, an anguished look on their face. We would be more patient and less judgmental when a friend or loved one fails to get over a broken heart in what we consider a timely manner. And when our own heart gets broken we would be more self-compassionate, feel less shameful about our distress, and more open to asking for the help we need.

For now though, we must remind ourselves that despite a lack of institutional support, we are not entirely defenseless against the psychological and physical assaults of heartbreak. There are things we can do (and things we should avoid doing) to ease our emotional pain, speed up our recovery, and heal the emotional and psychological wounds we suffered. Understanding what kinds of mistakes we must avoid and how to avoid getting stuck, and knowing what actions we should take and which habits to adopt in order to heal, means we are no longer at the mercy of the one curative ingredient over which we have no control—time. We can help our hearts heal and we can be more proactive and supportive in helping other broken hearts heal as well.

Heartbreak is all around us. It's time we open our eyes and see it, for only then can we truly heal it and move on.

REFERENCES

Bartels, Andreas, and Semir Zeki. "The Neural Basis of Romantic Love." *NeuroReport* 11, no. 17 (2000): 3829–34.

Baumeister, R. F., J. M. Twenge, and C. K. Nuss. "Effects of Social Exclusion on Cognitive Processes: Anticipated Aloneness Reduces Intelligent Thought." *Journal of Personality and Social Psychology* 83, no. 4 (2002): 817–27.

Boelen, Paul A., and Albert Reijntjes. "Negative Cognitions in Emotional Problems Following Romantic Relationship Break-ups." *Stress & Health* 25, no. 1 (2009): 11–19.

Breines, Juliana G., and Serena Chen. "Activating the Inner Caregiver: The Role of Support-Giving Schemas in Increasing State Self-Compassion." *Journal of Experimental Social Psychology* 49, no. 1 (2013): 58–64.

Cordaro, Millie. "Pet Loss and Disenfranchised Grief: Implications for Mental Health Counseling Practice." *Journal of Mental Health Counseling* 34, no. 4 (2012): 283–94.

Field, Tiffany. "Romantic Breakups, Heartbreak and Bereavement—Romantic Breakups." *Psychology* 2, no. 4 (2011): 382–87.

Fisher, Helen E., Xiaomeng Xu, Arthur Aron, and Lucy L. Brown. "Intense, Passionate, Romantic Love: A Natural Addiction? How the Fields That Investigate Romance and Substance Abuse Can Inform Each Other." *Frontiers in Psychology* 7:687 (2016).

Garimella, Kiran, Ingmar Weber, and Sonya Dal Cin. "From 'I Love You Babe' to 'Leave Me Alone'—Romantic Relationship Breakups on Twitter." 6th International Conference on Social Informatics (SocInfo 2014). Accessed online: arXiv:1409.5980 [cs.SI].

Keune, Philipp M., Vladimir Bostanov, Boris Kotchoubey, and Martin Hautzinger. "Mindfulness Versus Rumination and Behavioral Inhibition: A Perspective from Research on Frontal Brain Asymmetry." *Personality and Individual Differences* 53, no. 3 (2012): 323–28.

Knox, David, Marty E. Zusman, Melissa Kaluzny, and Chris Cooper. "College Student Recovery from a Broken Heart." *College Student Journal* 34 (2000): 322–24.

Kross, Ethan, Marc G. Berman, Walter Mischel, Edward E. Smith, and Tor D. Wager. "Social Rejection Shares Somatosensory Representations with Physical Pain." *Proceedings of the National Academy of Sciences* 108, no. 15 (2011): 6270–75.

"Broken Heart Syndrome." *Journal of the Association of Physicians of India* 64 (2016): 60–63.

Mason, Ashley E., Rita W. Law, Amanda E. B. Bryan, Robert M. Portley, and David A. Sbarra. "Facing a Breakup: Electromyographic Responses Moderate Self-Concept Recovery Following a Romantic Separation." *Personal Relationships* 19 (2012): 551–68.

Meloy, J. Reid, and Helen Fisher. "Some Thoughts on the Neurobiology of Stalking." *Journal of Forensic Sciences* 50, no. 6 (2005): 1472–80.

Robak, Rostyslaw W., and Steven P. Weitzman. "Grieving the Loss of Romantic Relationships in Young Adults: An Empirical Study of Disenfranchised Grief." *OMEGA: Journal of Death and Dying* 30, no. 4 (1995): 269–81.

Saffrey, Colleen, and Marion Ehrenberg. "When Thinking Hurts: Attachment, Rumination, and Postrelationship Adjustment." *Personal Relationships* 14, no. 3 (2007): 351–68.

## ACKNOWLEDGMENTS

I have worked with countless heartbroken people in my private practice for over two decades and so when Helen Walters, TED's editorial director (thank you, Helen!), and Michelle Quint, TED Books' executive editor, invited me to write a book about how to heal from heartbreak, I had two reactions. The first was to quickly say yes, and the second was to smack my forehead and wonder why I hadn't thought of that idea myself. Then I remembered that TED is all about great ideas, so it made sense they would be ahead of me on this one.

I got to work and quickly discovered what an amazing editor Michelle is. Thank you Michelle for making the process so collaborative and enjoyable from start to finish. Thanks also to the team at Simon & Schuster and to Henn Kim for her wonderful illustrations.

My wonderful agent, Michelle Tessler, always goes above and beyond the call of duty. I cannot thank her enough and feel so fortunate to have her represent me.

The first person who reads anything I write is always my twin brother, Dr. Gil Winch. His feedback, encouragement, and support were as invaluable and essential on this project as they always have been. I am also grateful to Efrat Winch, Brea Tremblay, Raquel D'Apice, Meghann Foye, Orli Zuravicky, and Jamie Parker for their insightful comments and suggestions. Lastly, I am eternally grateful to my patients. They come to me with open hearts and allow me into their deepest thoughts and feelings. It is a privilege I never take for granted and one from which I continue to learn and grow every day.

## ABOUT THE AUTHOR

Guy Winch, PhD, is a licensed psychologist, author, and keynote speaker whose books have been translated into twenty-three languages. His first TED Talk, *Why We All Need to Practice Emotional First Aid*, has been viewed more than five million times. Dr. Winch's work on the science of emotional health is frequently featured in national and international media outlets. He also writes the popular *Squeaky Wheel* blog for PsychologyToday.com. He maintains a private practice in Manhattan and is a member of the American Psychological Association.

Guy Winch's TED Talk, available for free at TED.com, is the companion to *How to Fix a Broken Heart*.

PHOTO: MARIA AUFMUTH/TED

### Brené Brown
*The Power of Vulnerability*
Brené Brown studies human connection — our ability to empathize, belong, and love. In a poignant, funny talk, she shares a deep insight from her research, one that sent her on a personal quest to know herself as well as to understand humanity. A talk to share.

### Andrew Solomon
*Depression, the Secret We Share*
"The opposite of depression is not happiness, but vitality, and it was vitality that seemed to seep away from me in that moment." In a talk equal parts eloquent and devastating, writer Andrew Solomon takes you to the darkest corners of his mind during the years he battled depression. That led him to an eye-opening journey across the world to interview others with depression — only to discover that, to his surprise, the more he talked, the more people wanted to tell their own stories.

### Helen Fisher
*The Brain in Love*
Why do we crave love so much, even to the point that we would die for it? To learn more about our very real, very physical need for romantic love, Helen Fisher and her research team took MRIs of people in love — and people who had just been dumped.

### Lidia Yuknavitch
*The Beauty of Being a Misfit*
To those who feel like they don't belong: there is beauty in being a misfit. Author Lidia Yuknavitch shares her own wayward journey in an intimate recollection of patchwork stories about loss, shame and the slow process of self-acceptance. "Even at the moment of your failure, you are beautiful," she says. "You don't know it yet, but you have the ability to reinvent yourself endlessly. That's your beauty."

**The Misfit's Manifesto**
by Lidia Yuknavitch

A misfit makes a powerful case for not fitting in—for recognizing the beauty, and difficulty, in forging an original path. Lidia Yuknavitch is a proud misfit. That wasn't always the case. It took Lidia a long time to not simply accept, but appreciate, her misfit status. *The Misfit's Manifesto* is for misfits around the world—the rebels, the eccentrics, the oddballs, and anyone who has ever felt like she was messing up.

**When Strangers Meet**
*How People You Don't Know Can Transform You*
by Kio Stark

Kio Stark invites you to discover the unexpected pleasures and exciting possibilities of talking to people you don't know. Stark reveals how these simple, surprising encounters push us toward greater openness and tolerance—and also how these fleeting but powerful emotional connections can change you and the world we share.

**The Great Questions of Tomorrow**
*The Ideas That Will Remake the World*
by David Rothkopf

We are on the cusp of a sweeping revolution—one that will change every facet of our lives. The changes ahead will challenge and alter fundamental concepts such as national identity, human rights, money and markets. In this pivotal, complicated moment, what are the great questions we need to ask to navigate our way forward?

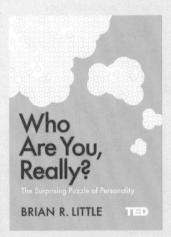

**Who Are You, Really?**
*The Surprising Puzzle of Personality*
by Brian R. Little

Who are you? Chances are you probably have a pretty fixed idea of what makes you, you. But what if your personality was flexible and ultimately in your control? Acclaimed psychologist Brian Little reveals that personality is far more malleable than we imagine.